Workshop on Annotating and Reasoning about Time and Events 2006

(ARTE)

Held in conjunction with COLING/ACL 2006

Sydney, Australia
23 July 2006

ISBN: 978-1-61738-505-6

Printed from e-media with permission by:

Curran Associates, Inc.
57 Morehouse Lane
Red Hook, NY 12571
www.proceedings.com

Some format issues inherent in the e-media version may also appear in this print version.

Printed by Curran Associates, Inc. (2010)

Association for Computational Linguistics
209 N. Eighth Street
Stroudsburg, Pennsylvania 18360

Phone: 1-570-476-8006
Fax: 1-570-476-0860

acl@aclweb.org

Table of Contents

Preface

Workshop Description

The computational analysis of time is a challenging and very topical problem, as the needs of applications based on information extraction techniques expand to include varying degrees of time stamping and temporal ordering of events and/or relations within a narrative. The challenges derive from the combined requirements of a mapping process (text to a rich representation of temporal entities), representational framework (ontologically-grounded temporal graph), and reasoning capability (combining commonsense inference with temporal axioms).

Usually contextualized in question-answering applications (with obvious dependencies of answers on time), temporal awareness directly impacts numerous areas of NLP and AI: text summarization over events and their participants; making inferences from events in a text; overlaying timelines on document collections; commonsense reasoning in narrative and story understanding.

Interest in temporal analysis and event-based reasoning has spawned a number of important meetings, particularly as applied to IE and QA tasks (cf. at COLING 2000; ACL 2001; LREC 2002; TERQAS 2002; TANGO 2003, Dagstuhl 2005). Significant progress has been made in these meetings, leading to developing a standard for a specification language for events and temporal expressions and their orderings (TimeML). While recent research in the broader community (as indicated, for instance, in the most recent symposium on Annotating and Reasoning about Time and Events) highlights TimeML's status as an interchange format, this workshop, however, is not intended to focus on TimeML exclusively. Likewise, while the ultimate goal of temporal analysis is to facilitate reasoning about time and events, the formal aspects of this problem are being addressed by other meetings (see, for instance, the TIME 2006 Symposium). Instead, the workshop will explore largely the linguistic implications for temporal-analytical frameworks.

The goal of the meeting, therefore, is to address issues already raised, but not fully explored – including but not limited to the following:

- infrastructure questions: temporal annotation methodology, tools; reliable measures of inter-annotator agreement; community resources.
- analytical frameworks: temporal information extraction; approaches to temporal expression normalization; relationship between named entity recognition and temporal entities analysis; dependency (or not) upon syntactic and discourse structure.
- mapping to time ontology(ies): completeness of the representation framework; formalization of the process; additional temporal reasoning capabilities required.
- reasoning over time: in particular, (robust) reasoning within representational schemes demonstrably derivable with current IE/analytical frameworks.
- applications of temporal analytics and reasoning: in addition to NL tasks, of particular interest are studies of temporal information as it manifests in, and impacts, different domains: beyond news, time is intrinsically essential in e.g., legal, health-care, intelligence, financial contexts.
- national language: relationship between language characteristics and representational frameworks; generalizations of temporal analytics across multiple languages; multi-/cross-lingual resource development.

Target Audience and Participants

This workshop will be of interest to those creating or exploiting temporally annotated corpora; those developing information extraction, question answering, and summarization systems relying on temporal and event ordering information; researchers involved in creating chronicles and timelines from textual data (legal, health-care, intelligence); semantic web designers and developers wanting to link web ontologies and standards to temporal markup from natural language; researchers interested in temporal properties of discourse and narrative structure; and those interested in annotation environments and development tools. For more details, refer to http://www.acl2006time.org.

Organizers

Chairs:

Branimir Boguraev, IBM T.J. Watson Research Center, USA
Rafael Munoz, University of Alicante, Spain
James Pustejovsky, Brandeis University, USA

Program Committee:

David Ahn, University of Amsterdam, The Netherlands
Nicholas Asher, University of Texas, Austin, TX USA
Paul Buitelaar, DFKI, Saarbruecken, Germany
Harry Bunt, Faculty of Arts, Tilburg University, The Netherlands
Corina Forascu, University of Iasi, Romania
Robert Gaizauskas, University of Sheffield, England
Jerry Hobbs, ISI/USC, Marina del Ray, CA USA
Graham Katz, University of Osnabrueck, Germany
Bernardo Magnini, ITC-IRST Trento, Italy
Inderjeet Mani, MITRE, Bedford, MA USA
Patricio Martinez-Barco, University of Alicante, Spain
Matteo Negri, ITC-IRST, Trento, Italy
Frank Schilder, Thomson Legal and Regulatory Co., Eagan, MN USA
Andrea Setzer, University of Sheffield, England
Marc Verhagen, Brandeis University, Waltham, MA USA

Workshop Program

Sunday, 23 July 2006

8:30–9:00	Opening Remarks, The Role of Standards in Temporal and Event Annotation James Pustejovsky, Branimir Boguraev and Rafael Munoz
9:00–9:45	*The stages of event extraction* David Ahn
9:45–10:30	*Local Semantics in the Interpretation of Temporal Expressions* Robert Dale and Pawel Mazur
10:30–11:00	Coffee Break
11:00–11:45	*Automatic Dating of Documents and Temporal Text Classification* Angelo Dalli and Yorick Wilks
11:45–12:30	*A Pilot Study on Acquiring Metric Temporal Constraints for Events* Inderjeet Mani and Ben Wellner
12:30–2:00	Lunch
2:00–2:45	*Evaluating Knowledge-based Approaches to the Multilingual Extension of a Temporal Expression Normalizer* Matteo Negri, Estela Saquete, Patricio Martínez-Barco and Rafael Muñoz
2:45–3:30	*Extending TimeML with Typical Durations of Events* Feng Pan, Rutu Mulkar and Jerry R. Hobbs
3:30–4:00	Coffee Break
4:00–4:45	*Marking Time in Developmental Biology: Annotating Developmental Events and their Links with Molecular Events* Gail Sinclair, Bonnie Webber and Duncan Davidson
4:45–5:45	Roadmap Discussion All

The stages of event extraction

David Ahn
Intelligent Systems Lab Amsterdam
University of Amsterdam
ahn@science.uva.nl

Abstract

Event detection and recognition is a complex task consisting of multiple sub-tasks of varying difficulty. In this paper, we present a simple, modular approach to event extraction that allows us to experiment with a variety of machine learning methods for these sub-tasks, as well as to evaluate the impact on performance these sub-tasks have on the overall task.

1 Introduction

Events are undeniably temporal entities, but they also possess a rich non-temporal structure that is important for intelligent information access systems (information retrieval, question answering, summarization, etc.). Without information about *what* happened, *where*, and to *whom*, temporal information about an event may not be very useful.

In the available annotated corpora geared toward information extraction, we see two models of events, emphasizing these different aspects. On the one hand, there is the TimeML model, in which an event is a word that points to a node in a network of temporal relations. On the other hand, there is the ACE model, in which an event is a complex structure, relating arguments that are themselves complex structures, but with only ancillary temporal information (in the form of temporal arguments, which are only noted when explicitly given). In the TimeML model, every event is annotated, because every event takes part in the temporal network. In the ACE model, only "interesting" events (events that fall into one of 34 predefined categories) are annotated.

The task of automatically extracting ACE events is more complex than extracting TimeML events (in line with the increased complexity of ACE events), involving detection of event anchors, assignment of an array of attributes, identification of arguments and assignment of roles, and determination of event coreference. In this paper, we present a modular system for ACE event detection and recognition. Our focus is on the difficulty and importance of each sub-task of the extraction task. To this end, we isolate and perform experiments on each stage, as well as evaluating the contribution of each stage to the overall task.

In the next section, we describe events in the ACE program in more detail. In section 3, we provide an overview of our approach and some information about our corpus. In sections 4 through 7, we describe our experiments for each of the subtasks of event extraction. In section 8, we compare the contribution of each stage to the overall task, and in section 9, we conclude.

2 Events in the ACE program

The ACE program[1] provides annotated data, evaluation tools, and periodic evaluation exercises for a variety of information extraction tasks. There are five basic kinds of extraction targets supported by ACE: entities, times, values, relations, and events. The ACE tasks for 2005 are more fully described in (ACE, 2005). In this paper, we focus on events, but since ACE events are complex structures involving entities, times, and values, we briefly describe these, as well.

ACE entities fall into seven types (person, organization, location, geo-political entity, facility, vehicle, weapon), each with a number of subtypes. Within the ACE program, a distinction is made between entities and entity mentions (similarly be-

[1] http://www.nist.gov/speech/tests/ace/

Proceedings of the Workshop on Annotating and Reasoning about Time and Events, pages 1–8,
Sydney, July 2006.

tween event and event mentions, and so on). An entity mention is a referring expression in text (a name, pronoun, or other noun phrase) that refers to something of an appropriate type. An entity, then, is either the actual referent, in the world, of an entity mention or the cluster of entity mentions in a text that refer to the same actual entity. The ACE Entity Detection and Recognition task requires both the identification of expressions in text that refer to entities (i.e., entity mentions) and coreference resolution to determine which entity mentions refer to the same entities.

There are also ACE tasks to detect and recognize times and a limited set of values (contact information, numeric values, job titles, crime types, and sentence types). Times are annotated according to the TIMEX2 standard, which requires normalization of temporal expressions (timexes) to an ISO-8601-like value.

ACE events, like ACE entities, are restricted to a range of types. Thus, not all events in a text are annotated—only those of an appropriate type. The eight event types (with subtypes in parentheses) are Life (Be-Born, Marry, Divorce, Injure, Die), Movement (Transport), Transaction (Transfer-Ownership, Transfer-Money), Business (Start-Org, Merge-Org, Declare-Bankruptcy, End-Org), Conflict (Attack, Demonstrate), Contact (Meet, Phone-Write), Personnel (Start-Position, End-Position, Nominate, Elect), Justice (Arrest-Jail, Release-Parole, Trial-Hearing, Charge-Indict, Sue, Convict, Sentence, Fine, Execute, Extradite, Acquit, Appeal, Pardon). Since there is nothing inherent in the task that requires the two levels of type and subtype, for the remainder of the paper, we will refer to the combination of event type and subtype (e.g., Life:Die) as the event type.

In addition to their type, events have four other attributes (possible values in parentheses): modality (Asserted, Other), polarity (Positive, Negative), genericity (Specific, Generic), tense (Past, Present, Future, Unspecified).

The most distinctive characteristic of events (unlike entities, times, and values, but like relations) is that they have arguments. Each event type has a set of possible argument roles, which may be filled by entities, values, or times. In all, there are 35 role types, although no single event can have all 35 roles. A complete description of which roles go with which event types can be found in the annotation guidelines for ACE events (LDC, 2005).

Events, like entities, are distinguished from their mentions in text. An event mention is a span of text (an *extent*, usually a sentence) with a distinguished *anchor* (the word that "most clearly expresses [an event's] occurrence" (LDC, 2005)) and zero or more arguments, which are entity mentions, timexes, or values in the extent. An event is either an actual event, in the world, or a cluster of event mentions that refer to the same actual event. Note that the arguments of an event are the entities, times, and values corresponding to the entity mentions, timexes, and values that are arguments of the event mentions that make up the event.

The official evaluation metric of the ACE program is ACE value, a cost-based metric which associates a normalized, weighted cost to system errors and subtracts that cost from a maximum score of 100%. For events, the associated costs are largely determined by the costs of the arguments, so that errors in entity, timex, and value recognition are multiplied in event ACE value. Since it is useful to evaluate the performance of event detection and recognition independently of the recognition of entities, times, and values, the ACE program includes diagnostic tasks, in which partial ground truth information is provided. Of particular interest here is the diagnostic task for event detection and recognition, in which ground truth entities, values, and times are provided. For the remainder of this paper, we use this diagnostic methodology, and we extend it to sub-tasks within the task, evaluating components of our event recognition system using ground truth output of upstream components. Furthermore, in our evaluating our system components, we use the more transparent metrics of precision, recall, F-measure, and accuracy.

3 Our approach to event extraction

3.1 A pipeline for detecting and recognizing events

Extracting ACE events is a complex task. Our goal with the approach we describe in this paper is to establish baseline performance in this task using a relatively simple, modular system. We break down the task of extracting events into a series of classification sub-tasks, each of which is handled by a machine-learned classifier.

1. Anchor identification: finding event anchors (the basis for event mentions) in text and assigning them an event type;

2. Argument identification: determining which entity mentions, timexes, and values are arguments of each event mention;

3. Attribute assignment: determining the values of the modality, polarity, genericity, and tense attributes for each event mention;

4. Event coreference: determining which event mentions refer to the same event.

In principle, these four sub-tasks are highly interdependent, but for the approach described here, we do not model all these dependencies. Anchor identification is treated as an independent task. Argument finding and attribute assignment are each dependent only on the results of anchor identification, while event coreference depends on the results of all of the other three sub-tasks.

To learn classifiers for the first three tasks, we experiment with TiMBL[2], a memory-based (nearest neighbor) learner (Daelemans et al., 2004), and MegaM[3], a maximum entropy learner (Daumé III, 2004). For event coreference, we use only MegaM, since our approach requires probabilities. In addition to comparing the performance of these two learners on the various sub-tasks, we also experiment with the structure of the learning problems for the first two tasks.

In the remainder of this paper, we present experiments for each of these sub-tasks (sections 4– 7), focusing on each task in isolation, and then look at how the sub-tasks affect performance in the overall task (section 8). First, we discuss the preprocessing of the corpus required for our experiments.

3.2 Preprocessing the corpus

Because of restrictions imposed by the organizers on the 2005 ACE program data, we use only the ACE 2005 training corpus, which contains 599 documents, for our experiments. We split this corpus into training and test sets at the document-level, with 539 training documents and 60 test documents. From the training set, another 60 documents are reserved as a development set, which is used for parameter tuning by MegaM. For the remainder of the paper, we will refer to the 539 training documents as the training corpus and the 60 test documents as the test corpus.

For our machine learning experiments, we need a range of information in order to build feature vectors. Since we are interested only in performance on event extraction, we follow the methodology of the ACE diagnostic tasks and use the ground truth entity, timex2, and value annotations both for training and testing. Additionally, each document is tokenized and split into sentences using a simple algorithm adapted from (Grefenstette, 1994, p. 149). These sentences are parsed using the August 2005 release of the Charniak parser (Charniak, 2000)[4]. The parses are converted into dependency relations using a method similar to (Collins, 1999; Jijkoun and de Rijke, 2004). The syntactic annotations thus provide access both to constituency and dependency information. Note that with respect to these two sources of syntactic information, we use the word *head* ambiguously to refer both to the head of a constituent (i.e., the distinguished word within the constituent from which the constituent inherits its category features) and to the head of a dependency relation (i.e., the word on which the dependent in the relation depends).

Since parses and entity/timex/value annotations are produced independently, we need a strategy for matching (entity/timex/value) mentions to parses. Given a mention, we first try to find a single constituent whose offsets exactly match the extent of the mention. In the training and development data, there is an exact-match constituent for 89.2% of the entity mentions. If there is no such constituent, we look for a sequence of constituents that match the mention extent. If there is no such sequence, we back off to a single word, looking first for a word whose start offset matches the start of the mention, then for a word whose end offset matches the end of the mention, and finally for a word that contains the entire mention. If all these strategies fail, then no parse information is provided for the mention. Note that when a mention matches a sequence of constituents, the head of the constituent in the sequence that is shallowest in the parse tree is taken to be the (constituent) head of the entire sequence. Given a parse constituent, we take the entity type of that constituent to be the type of the smallest entity mention overlapping with it.

4 Identifying event anchors

4.1 Task structure

We model anchor identification as a word classification task. Although an event anchor may in principle be more than one word, more than 95% of

[2] `http://ilk.uvt.nl/timbl/`

[3] `http://www.isi.edu/~hdaume/megam/`

[4] `ftp://ftp.cs.brown.edu/pub/nlparser/`

the anchors in the training data consist of a single word. Furthermore, in the training data, anchors are restricted in part of speech (to nouns: NN, NNS, NNP; verbs: VB, VBZ, VBP, VBG, VBN, VBD, AUX, AUXG, MD; adjectives: JJ; adverbs: RB, WRB; pronouns: PRP, WP; determiners: DT, WDT, CD; and prepositions: IN). Thus, anchor identification for a document is reduced to the task of classifying each word in the document with an appropriate POS tag into one of 34 classes (the 33 event types plus a None class for words that are not an event anchor).

The class distribution for these 34 classes is heavily skewed. In the 202,135 instances in the training data, the None class has 197,261 instances, while the next largest class (Conflict:Attack) has only 1410 instances. Thus, in addition to modeling anchor identification as a single multi-class classification task, we also try to break down the problem into two stages: first, a binary classifier that determines whether or not a word is an anchor, and then, a multi-class classifier that determines the event type for the positive instances from the first task. For this staged task, we train the second classifier on the ground truth positive instances.

4.2 Features for event anchors

We use the following set of features for all configurations of our anchor identification experiments.

- Lexical features: full word, lowercase word, lemmatized word, POS tag, depth of word in parse tree
- WordNet features: for each WordNet POS category c (from N, V, ADJ, ADV):
  - If the word is in catgory c and there is a corresponding WordNet entry, the ID of the synset of first sense is a feature value
  - Otherwise, if the word has an entry in WordNet that is morphologically related to a synset of category c, the ID of the related synset is a feature value
- Left context (3 words): lowercase, POS tag
- Right context (3 words): lowercase, POS tag
- Dependency features: if the candidate word is the dependent in a dependency relation, the label of the relation is a feature value, as are the dependency head word, its POS tag, and its entity type
- Related entity features: for each entity/timex/value type t:
  - Number of dependents of candidate word of type t
  - Label(s) of dependency relation(s) to dependent(s) of type t
  - Constituent head word(s) of dependent(s) of type t
  - Number of entity mentions of type t reachable by some dependency path (i.e., in same sentence)
  - Length of path to closest entity mention of type t

4.3 Results

In table 1, we present the results of our anchor classification experiments (precision, recall and F-measure). The all-at-once conditions refer to experiments with a single multi-class classifier (using either MegaM or TiMBL), while the split conditions refer to experiments with two staged classifiers, where we experiment with using MegaM and TiMBL for both classifiers, as well as with using MegaM for the binary classification and TiMBL for the multi-class classification. In table 2, we present the results of the two first-stage binary classifiers, and in table 3, we present the results of the two second-stage multi-class classifiers on ground truth positive instances. Note that we always use the default parameter settings for MegaM, while for TiMBL, we set k (number of neighbors to consider) to 5, we use inverse distance weighting for the neighbors and weighted overlap, with information gain weighting, for all non-numeric features.

Both for the all-at-once condition and for multi-class classification of positive instances, the nearest neighbor classifier performs substantially better than the maximum entropy classifier. For binary classification, though, the two methods perform similarly, and staging either binary classifier with the nearest neighbor classifier for positive instances yields the best results. In practical terms, using the maximum entropy classifier for binary classification and then the TiMBL classifier to classify only the positive instances is the best solution, since classification with TiMBL tends to be slow.

	Precision	Recall	F
All-at-once/megam	0.691	0.239	0.355
All-at-once/timbl	0.666	0.540	0.596
Split/megam	0.589	0.417	0.489
Split/timbl	0.657	0.551	0.599
Split/megam+timbl	0.725	0.513	0.601

Table 1: Results for anchor detection and classification

	Precision	Recall	F
Binary/megam	0.756	0.535	0.626
Binary/timbl	0.685	0.574	0.625

Table 2: Results for anchor detection (i.e., binary classification of anchor instances)

5 Argument identification

5.1 Task structure

Identifying event arguments is a pair classification task. Each event mention is paired with each of the entity/timex/value mentions occurring in the same sentence to form a single classification instance. There are 36 classes in total: 35 role types and a None class. Again, the distribution of classes is skewed, though not as heavily as for the anchor task, with 20,556 None instances out of 29,450 training instances. One additional consideration is that no single event type allows arguments of all 36 possible roles; each event type has its own set of allowable roles. With this in mind, we experiment with treating argument identification as a single multi-class classification task and with training a separate multi-class classifier for each event type. Note that all classifiers are trained using ground truth event mentions.

5.2 Features for argument identification

We use the following set of features for all our argument classifiers.

- Anchor word of event mention: full, lowercase, POS tag, and depth in parse tree

	Accuracy
Multi/megam	0.649
Multi/timbl	0.824

Table 3: Accuracy for anchor classification (i.e., multi-class classification of positive anchor instances)

	Precision	Recall	F
All-at-once/megam	0.708	0.430	0.535
All-at-once/timbl	0.509	0.453	0.480
CPET/megam	0.689	0.490	0.573
CPET/timbl	0.504	0.535	0.519

Table 4: Results for arguments

- Event type of event mention
- Constituent head word of entity mention: full, lowercase, POS tag, and depth in parse tree
- Determiner of entity mention, if any
- Entity type and mention type (name, pronoun, other NP) of entity mention
- Dependency path between anchor word and constituent head word of entity mention, expressed as a sequence of labels, of words, and of POS tags

5.3 Results

In table 4, we present the results for argument identification. The all-at-once conditions refer to experiments with a single classifier for all instances. The CPET conditions refer to experiments with a separate classifier for each event type. Note that we use the same parameter settings for MegaM and TiMBL as for anchor classification, except that for TiMBL, we use the modified value difference metric for the three dependency path features.

Note that splitting the task into separate tasks for each event type yields a substantial improvement over using a single classifier. Unlike in the anchor classification task, maximum entropy classification handily outperforms nearest-neighbor classification. This may be related to the binarization of the dependency-path features for maximum entropy training: the word and POS tag sequences (but not the label sequences) are broken down into their component steps, so that there is a separate binary feature corresponding to the presence of a given word or POS tag in the dependency path.

Table 5 presents results of each of the classifiers restricted to Time-* arguments (Time-Within, Time-Holds, etc.). These arguments are of particular interest not only because they provide the link between events and times in this model of events, but also because Time-* roles, unlike other role

	Precision	Recall	F
All-at-once/megam	0.688	0.477	0.564
All-at-once/timbl	0.500	0.482	0.491
CPET/megam	0.725	0.451	0.556
CPET/timbl	0.357	0.404	0.379

Table 5: Results for Time-* arguments

	Accuracy
megam	0.795
timbl	0.793
baseline	0.802
majority (in training)	0.773

Table 6: Genericity

types, are available to all event types. We see that, in fact, the all-at-once classifiers perform better for these role types, which suggests that it may be worthwhile to factor out these role types and build a classifier specifically for temporal arguments.

6 Assigning attributes

6.1 Task structure

In addition to the event type and subtype attributes, (the event associated with) each event mention must also be assigned values for genericity, modality, polarity, and tense. We train a separate classifier for each attribute. Genericity, modality, and polarity are each binary classification tasks, while tense is a multi-class task. We use the same features as for the anchor identification task, with the exception of the lemmatized anchor word and the WordNet features.

6.2 Results

The results of our classification experiments are given in tables 6, 7, 8, and 9. Note that modality, polarity, and genericity are skewed tasks where it is difficult to improve on the baseline majority classification (Asserted, Positive, and Specific, respectively) and where maximum entropy and nearest neighbor classification perform very similarly. For tense, however, both learned classifiers perform substantially better than the majority baseline (Past), with the maximum entropy classifier providing the best performance.

	Accuracy
megam	0.750
timbl	0.759
baseline	0.738
majority (in training)	0.749

Table 7: Modality

	Accuracy
megam	0.955
timbl	0.955
baseline	0.950
majority (in training)	0.967

Table 8: Polarity

7 Event coreference

7.1 Task structure

For event coreference, we follow the approach to entity coreference detailed in (Florian et al., 2004). This approach uses a mention-pair coreference model with probabilistic decoding. Each event mention in a document is paired with every other event mention, and a classifier assigns to each pair of mentions the probability that the paired mentions corefer. These probabilities are used in a left-to-right entity linking algorithm in which each mention is compared with all already-established events (i.e., event mention clusters) to determine whether it should be added to an existing event or start a new one. Since the classifier needs to output probabilities for this approach, we do not use TiMBL, but only train a maximum entropy classifier with MegaM.

7.2 Features for coreference classification

We use the following set of features for our mention-pair classifier. The *candidate* is the earlier event mention in the text, and the *anaphor* is the later mention.

- *CandidateAnchor+AnaphorAnchor*, also POS tag and lowercase

	Accuracy
megam	0.633
timbl	0.613
baseline	0.535
majority (in training)	0.512

Table 9: Tense

	Precision	Recall	F
megam	0.761	0.580	0.658
baseline	0.167	1.0	0.286

Table 10: Coreference

- *CandidateEventType+AnaphorEventType*
- Depth of candidate anchor word in parse tree
- Depth of anaphor anchor word in parse tree
- Distance between candidate and anchor, measured in sentences
- Number, heads, and roles of shared arguments (same entity/timex/value w/same role)
- Number, heads, and roles of candidate arguments that are not anaphor arguments
- Number, heads, and roles of anaphor arguments that are not candidate arguments
- Heads and roles of arguments shared by candidate and anaphor in different roles
- *CandidateModalityVal+AnaphorModalityVal*, also for polarity, genericity, and tense

7.3 Results

In table 10, we present the performance of our event coreference pair classifier. Note that the distribution for this task is also skewed: only 3092 positive instances of 42,736 total training instances. Simple baseline of taking event mentions of identical type to be coreferent does quite poorly.

8 Evaluation with ACE value

Table 11 presents results of performing the full event detection and recognition task, swapping in ground truth (gold) or learned classifiers (learned) for the various sub-tasks (we also swap in majority classifiers for the attribute sub-task). For the anchor sub-task, we use the split/megam+timbl classifier; for the argument sub-task, we use the CPET/megam classifier; for the attribute sub-tasks, we use the megam classifiers; for the coreference sub-task, we use the approach outlined in section 7. Since in our approach, the argument and attribute sub-tasks are dependent on the anchor sub-task and the coreference sub-task is dependent on all of the other sub-tasks, we cannot freely swap in ground truth—e.g., if we use a learned classifier for the anchor sub-task, then there is no ground truth for the corresponding argument and attribute sub-tasks.

The learned coreference classifier provides a small boost to performance over doing no coreference at all (7.5% points for the condition in which all the other sub-tasks use ground truth (1 vs. 8), 0.6% points when all the other sub-tasks use learned classifiers (7 vs. 12)). From perfect coreference, using ground truth for the other subtasks, the loss in value is 11.4% points (recall that maximum ACE value is 100%). Note that the difference between perfect coreference and no coreference is only 18.9% points.

Looking at the attribute sub-tasks, the effects on ACE value are even smaller. Using the learned attribute classifiers (with ground truth anchors and arguments) results in 4.8% point loss in value from ground truth attributes (1 vs. 5) and only a 0.5% point gain in value from majority class attributes (4 vs. 5). With learned anchors and arguments, the learned attribute classifiers result in a 0.4% loss in value from even majority class attributes (3 vs. 7).

Arguments clearly have the greatest impact on ACE value (which is unsurprising, given that arguments are weighted heavily in event value). Using ground truth anchors and attributes, learned arguments result in a loss of value of 35.6% points from ground truth arguments (1 vs. 2). When the learned coreference classifier is used, the loss in value from ground truth arguments to learned arguments is even greater (42.5%, 8 vs. 10).

Anchor identification also has a large impact on ACE value. Without coreference but with learned arguments and attributes, the difference between using ground truth anchors and learned anchors is 22.2% points (6 vs. 7). With coreference, the difference is still 21.0% points (11 vs. 12).

Overall, using the best learned classifiers for the various subtasks, we achieve an ACE value score of 22.3%, which falls within the range of scores for the 2005 diagnostic event extraction task (19.7%–32.7%).[5] Note, though, that these scores are not really comparable, since they involve training on the full training set and testing on a separate set of documents (as noted above, the 2005 ACE testing data is not available for further experimentation, so we are using 90% of the original training data for training/development and

[5]For the diagnostic task, ground truth entities, values, and times, are provided, as they are in our experiments.

	anchors	args	attrs	coref	ACE value
1	gold	gold	gold	none	81.1%
2	gold	learned	gold	none	45.5%
3	learned	learned	maj	none	22.1%
4	gold	gold	maj	none	75.8%
5	gold	gold	learned	none	76.3%
6	gold	learned	learned	none	43.9%
7	learned	learned	learned	none	21.7%
8	gold	gold	gold	learned	88.6%
9	gold	gold	learned	learned	79.4%
10	gold	learned	gold	learned	46.1%
11	gold	learned	learned	learned	43.3%
12	learned	learned	learned	learned	22.3%

Table 11: ACE value

10% for the results presented here).

9 Conclusion and future work

In this paper, we have presented a system for ACE event extraction. Even with the simple breakdown of the task embodied by the system and the limited feature engineering for the machine learned classifiers, the performance is not too far from the level of the best systems at the 2005 ACE evaluation. Our approach is modular, and it has allowed us to present several sets of experiments exploring the effect of different machine learning algorithms on the sub-tasks and exploring the effect of the different sub-tasks on the overall performance (as measured by ACE value).

There is clearly a great deal of room for improvement. As we have seen, improving anchor and argument identification will have the greatest impact on overall performance, and the experiments we have done suggest directions for such improvement. For anchor identification, taking one more step toward binary classification and training a binary classifier for each event type (either for all candidate anchor instances or only for positive instances) may be helpful. For argument identification, we have already discussed the idea of modeling temporal arguments separately; perhaps introducing a separate classifier for each role type might also be helpful.

For all the sub-tasks, there is more feature engineering that could be done (a simple example: for coreference, boolean features corresponding to identical anchors and event types). Furthermore, the dependencies between sub-tasks could be better modeled.

References

2005. The ACE 2005 (ACE05) evaluation plan. `http://www.nist.gov/speech/tests/ace/ace05/doc/ace05-evalplan.v3.pdf`.

Eugene Charniak. 2000. A maximum-entropy-inspired parser. In *Proceedings of the 1st Meeting of NAACL*, pages 132–139.

Michael Collins. 1999. *Head-Driven Statistical Models for Natural Language Parsing*. Ph.D. thesis, University of Pennsylvania.

Walter Daelemans, Jakub Zavrel, Ko van der Sloot, and Antal van den Bosch. 2004. *TiMBL: Tilburg Memory Based Learner, version 5.1, Reference Guide*. University of Tilburg, ILK Technical Report ILK-0402. http://ilk.uvt.nl/.

Hal Daumé III. 2004. Notes on CG and LM-BFGS optimization of logistic regression. Paper available at `http://www.isi.edu/~hdaume/docs/daume04cg-bfgs.ps`, August.

Radu Florian, Hany Hassan, Abraham Ittycheriah, Hongyan Jing, Nanda Kambhatla, Xiaoqiang Luo, Nicolas Nicolov, and Salim Roukos. 2004. A statistical model for multilingual entity detection and tracking. In *Proceedings of HLT/NAACL-04*.

Gregory Grefenstette. 1994. *Explorations in Automatic Thesaurus Discovery*. Kluwer.

Valentin Jijkoun and Maarten de Rijke. 2004. Enriching the output of a parser using memory-based learning. In *Proceedings of the 42nd Meeting of the ACL*.

Linguistic Data Consortium, 2005. *ACE (Automatic Content Extraction) English Annotation Guidelines for Events*, version 5.4.3 2005.07.01 edition.

Local Semantics in the Interpretation of Temporal Expressions

Robert Dale* **and Paweł Mazur**†
Centre for Language Technology
Macquarie University, NSW 2109, Sydney, Australia
*Robert.Dale@mq.edu.au,
†mpawel@ics.mq.edu.au

Abstract

Work on the interpretation of temporal expressions in text has generally been pursued in one of two paradigms: the formal semantics approach, where an attempt is made to provide a well-grounded theoretical basis for the interpretation of these expressions, and the more pragmatically-focused approach represented by the development of the TIMEX2 standard, with its origins in work in information extraction. The former emphasises formal elegance and consistency; the latter emphasises broad coverage for practical applications. In this paper, we report on the development of a framework that attempts to integrate insights from both perspectives, with the aim of achieving broad coverage of the domain in a well-grounded manner from a formal perspective. We focus in particular on the development of a compact notation for representing the semantics of underspecified temporal expressions that can be used to provide component-level evaluation of systems that interpret such expressions.

1 Introduction

Obtaining a precise semantic representation for utterances related to time is interesting both from a theoretical point of view, as there are many complex phenomena to be addressed, and for purely practical applications such as information extraction, question answering, or the ordering of events on a timeline.

In the literature, work on the interpretation of temporal expressions comes from two directions. On the one hand, work in formal semantics (see, for example, (Pratt and Francez, 2001)) aims to provide a formally well-grounded approach to the representation of the semantics of these expressions, but such approaches are difficult to scale up to the broad coverage required for practical applications; on the other hand, work that has its roots in information extraction, while it emphasizes broad coverage, often results in the use of ad hoc representations. The most developed work in this direction is focused around the TimeML markup language[1] (described, for example, in (Pustejovsky et al., 2003) and in the collection edited by Mani et al. (2005)).

Some work attempts to bring these two traditions together: notable in this respect is Schilder's (2004) work on temporal expressions in German newswire text, and Hobbs and Pan's (2004) work on the axiomatisation in terms of OWL-Time. Saquete et al. (2002) present an approach that views time expressions as anaphoric references.

We take the view that an important step towards a truly broad coverage yet semantically well-founded approach is to recognize that there is a principled distinction to be made between the interpretation of the semantics of a temporal expression devoid of its context of use, and the fuller interpretation of that expression when the context is taken into account. The first of these, which we refer to here as the **local semantics** of a temporal expression, should be derivable in a compositional manner from the components of the expression; determining the value of the second, which we refer to as the **global semantics** of the expression, may require arbitrary inference and reason-

[1]Note that with TimeML one can annotate not only temporal expressions, but also events and relations between events and temporal expressions.

Proceedings of the Workshop on Annotating and Reasoning about Time and Events, pages 9–16,
Sydney, July 2006.

ing. Such a distinction is implicit in other accounts: Schilder's (2004) use of lambda expressions allows representation of partially specified temporal entities, and the temporary variables that Negri and Marseglia (2005) construct during the interpretation of a given temporal expression capture something of the same notion.

Our proposal here is to reify this level of intermediate representation based on a formalization in terms of recursive attribute–value matrices. This has two distinct advantages: it provides a convenient representation of underspecification, and it leads naturally to a compositional approach to the construction of the semantics of temporal expressions via unification. We also provide a compact encoding of this representation that is essentially an extension of the existing TIMEX2 representation for temporal expressions. This brings the advantages that (a) existing tools and machinery for evaluation can be used to determine how well a given implementation derives these local semantic values; and (b) performance in the determination of local semantics and global semantics can be tested independently. To ensure breadth of coverage, we have developed our representation on the basis of the 256 examples of temporal expressions provided in the TIMEX2 guidelines (Ferro et al., 2005). To make it possible to compare systems on their performance in producing these intermediate representations, we make available this set of examples annotated in-line with the representations described here.

The rest of this paper is structured as follows. In Section 2, we describe the architecture of DANTE, a system which embodies our approach to the detection and normalisation of temporal expressions; in particular, we focus on the architecture employed in this approach, and on the particular levels of representation that it makes use of. In Section 3, we argue for an intermediate representational level that captures the semantics of temporal expressions independent of the context of their interpretation, and introduce the idea of using recursive attribute–value matrices to represent the semantics of temporal expressions. In Section 4, we provide an encoding of these attribute–value matrices in a compact string-based representation that is effectively an extension of the ISO-based date–time format representations used in the TIMEX2 standard, thus enabling easy evaluation of system performance using existing tools. In Section 5 we discuss how the approach handles constructions that contain one TIMEX embedded within another. Finally, in Section 6 we draw some conclusions and point to future work.

2 The DANTE System

2.1 Processing Steps

In our work, our goal is very close to that for which the TIMEX2 standard was developed: we want to annotate each temporal expression in a document with an indication of its interpretation, in the form of an extended ISO-format date and time string, normalised to some time zone. So, for example, suppose we have the following italicised temporal expression in an email message that was sent from Sydney on Monday 10th April 2006:

(1) I expect that we will be able to present this at the meeting on *Friday at 11am*.

In the context of our application, this temporal expression should be marked up as follows:

(2)
```
<TIMEX2 VAL="2006-04-14T01:00GMT">
Friday at 11am</TIMEX2>
```

We have to do three things to achieve the desired result:

- First, we have to detect the extent of the temporal expression in the text. We refer to this process as **temporal expression recognition**.
- Then, we have to use information from the document context to turn the recognized expression into a fully specified date and time. We refer to this as **temporal expression interpretation**.
- Finally, we have to normalise this fully specified date and time to a predefined time zone, which in the case of the present example is Greenwich Mean Time. We refer to this as **temporal expression normalisation**.[2]

[2]Note that this third step is not required by the TIMEX guidelines, but is an additional requirement in the context of our particular application. This also means that our use of the term 'normalisation' here is not consistent with the standard usage in the TIMEX context; however, we would argue that our distinction between interpretation and normalisation describes more accurately the nature of the processes involved here.

We observe that, at the time that the extent of a temporal expression within a text is determined, it is also possible to derive some semantic representation of that expression irrespective of the wider context within which it needs to be interpreted: for example, by virtue of having recognized an occurrence of the string *Friday* in a text, we already know that this is a reference to a specific day of the week. Most existing systems for the interpretation of temporal expressions probably make use of such a level of representation. Schilder's (2004) approach captures the semantics here in terms of a lambda expression like $\lambda x \text{Friday}(x)$; Negri and Marseglia (2005) capture information at this stage of processing via a collection of temporary attributes.

In our system, each of the three steps above corresponds to a distinct processing component in the DANTE system architecture. These components communicate in terms of a number of distinct representations, which we now describe.

2.2 The Text

This level of representation corresponds simply to the strings that constitute temporal expressions in text. These are understood to be linguistic constructions whose referents are entities in the temporal domain: either points in time, or periods of time. In the above example, the text representation is simply the string *Friday at 11am.*

2.3 Local Semantics

We use this term to refer to a level of representation that corresponds to the semantic content that is derivable directly from the text representation; in the case of temporal expressions that are arguments to prepositions, this includes the interpretation of the preposition. Such representations are often incomplete, in that they do not denote a particular point or period on the time line; however, usually they do partially specify points or periods, and constrain the further interpretation of the string.

2.4 In-Document Semantics

We use this term to refer to the fully explicit interpretation of the text string, to the extent that this can be determined from the document itself, in conjunction with any metadata associated with the document. This level of representation corresponds to the information encoded in the attributes of the TIMEX2 tag as defined in the TIMEX guidelines.

2.5 Global Semantics

The TIMEX guidelines do not have anything to say beyond the representation described in the previous section. In our application, however, we are also required to normalise all temporal expressions to a specific time zone. This requires that some further temporal arithmetic be applied to the semantics of the found expressions. To calculate this, we simply have to determine the difference between the time zone of the document containing the temporal reference and the target time zone, here Greenwich Mean Time. The document may not always be explicitly marked with information about the time zone of its creation; in such cases, this has to be inferred from information about the location of the author or sender of the message.

3 Representing Temporal Expressions

In this section, we describe a conceptualisation of the semantics of temporal expressions in terms of recursive attribute–value matrices.

3.1 Temporal Entities

As is conventional in this area of research, we view the temporal world as consisting of two basic types of entities, these being **points in time** and **durations**; each of these has an internal hierarchical structure. We can represent these in the following manner:[3]

```
[point
 TIMEANDDATE [TIME [HOUR 15
                    MINS 00
                    SECS 00]
              DATE [DAY   [DAYNAME D4
                           DAYNUM  13]
                    MONTH 5
                    YEAR  2006]]
 ZONE Z]
```

The example above corresponds to the semantics of the temporal expression *3pm Thursday 13th May 2006 GMT*; in the ISO date and time format used in the TIMEX2 standard, this would be written as follows:

(3) `2006-05-13T15:00:00Z`

[3]For reasons of limitations of space, we will ignore durations in the present discussion; their representation is similar in spirit to the examples provided here.

Each atomic feature in the attribute–value structure thus corresponds to a specific position in the ISO format date–time string.

3.2 Underspecification

Of course, very few temporal expressions in text are fully specified. The attribute–value matrix representation makes it easy to represent the content of underspecified temporal expressions. For example, the content of the temporal expression *Thursday* in a sentence like *We will meet on Thursday* can be expressed as follows:

$$\begin{bmatrix} \textit{point} & \\ \text{TIMEANDDATE} & \begin{bmatrix} \text{DATE} & \begin{bmatrix} \text{DAY} & \begin{bmatrix} \text{DAYNAME} & \textit{D4} \end{bmatrix} \end{bmatrix} \end{bmatrix} \end{bmatrix}$$

On the other hand, a reference to *13th May* in a sentence like *We will meet on 13th May* has this representation:

$$\begin{bmatrix} \textit{point} & \\ \text{TIMEANDDATE} & \begin{bmatrix} \text{DATE} & \begin{bmatrix} \text{DAY} & \begin{bmatrix} \text{DAYNUM} & \textit{13} \end{bmatrix} \\ \text{MONTH} & \textit{05} \end{bmatrix} \end{bmatrix} \end{bmatrix}$$

In the cases just described, the semantic representation corresponds to the entire temporal noun phrase in each case. The same form of representation is easy to use in a compositional semantic framework: each constituent in a larger temporal expression provides a structure that can be unified with the structures corresponding to the other constituents of the expression to provide a semantics for the expression as a whole. The values of the atomic elements in such an expression come from the lexicon; multiword sequences that are best considered atomic (such as, for example, idioms) can also be assigned semantic representations in the same way. The value of a composite structure is produced by unifying the values of its constituents. Unifying the two structures above, for example, gives us the following representation for *Thursday 13th May*:[4]

$$\begin{bmatrix} \textit{point} & \\ \text{TIMEANDDATE} & \begin{bmatrix} \text{DATE} & \begin{bmatrix} \text{DAY} & \begin{bmatrix} \text{DAYNAME} & \textit{D4} \\ \text{DAYNUM} & \textit{13} \end{bmatrix} \\ \text{MONTH} & \textit{05} \end{bmatrix} \end{bmatrix} \end{bmatrix}$$

So, these structures provide a convenient representation for what we have referred to above as the local semantics of a temporal expression, and correspond to the output of the recognition stage of our processing architecture.

3.3 Interpretation

We can now define the task of interpretation in terms of the content of these structures. We assume a **granularity ordering** over what we might think of as the **defining attributes** in a temporal representation:

(4) year > month > daynum > hour > minute > second

These are, of course, precisely the elements that are represented explicitly in an ISO date–time expression.

Interpretation of a partially specified temporal expression then requires ensuring that there is a value for every defining attribute that is of greater granularity than the smallest granularity present in the partially specified representation. We refer to this as the **granularity rule** in interpretation.

In the case of the example in the previous section, the granularity rule tells us that in order to compute the full semantic value of the expression we have to determine a value for YEAR, but not for HOUR, MINS or SECS. This interpretation process may require a variety of forms of reasoning and inference, as discussed below, and is qualitatively different from the computation of the local semantics.

In the context of our application, a third stage, the normalisation process, then requires taking the further step of adding a ZONE attribute with a specific value, and translating the rest of the construction into this time zone if it represents a time in another time zone.

4 A Compact Encoding

The structures described in the previous section are relatively unwieldy in comparison to the simple string structures used as values in the TIMEX standard. To enable easy evaluation of a system's ability to construct these intermediate semantic representations, we would like to use a representation that is immediately usable by existing evaluation tools. To achieve this goal, we define a number of extensions to the standard TIMEX2 string representation for values of the VAL attribute; these extensions allow us to capture the range of distinctions we need. To save space, we

[4] For simplicity here we assume that the syntactic structure of such an expression is captured by the context-free grammar rule 'NP → NP NP'. Other treatments are possible.

also use these representations here to show the coverage of the annotation scheme that results.

In our implementation, we represent the local semantic content via an additional set of attributes on TIMEX elements that mirrors exactly the set of attributes used by the TIMEX2 standard: thus we have T-VAL, T-ANCHOR_VAL and so on. This means that markup applied to a text distinguishes intermediate and final semantic values, making it possible to evaluate on just intermediate values, just final values, or both. In what follows, we will also use these intermediate attributes to make clear which level of representation is under discussion.

4.1 Partially Specified Dates and Times

As noted above, many references to dates or times are not fully specified in a text, with the result that some parts will have to be computed from the context during the interpretation stage. Typical examples are as follows:

(5) a. We'll see you in *November*.

b. I expect to see you at *half past eight*.

In the recursive attribute–value notation introduced above, the missing information in each case corresponds to those features that are absent in the structure as determined by the granularity rule introduced in Section 3.3.

In our string-based notation, we use lowercase xs to indicate those elements for which a value needs to be found, but which are not available at the time the local semantics are computed; and we capture the granularity requirement by omitting from the string representation those elements that do not require a value.[5] Table 1 provides a range of examples that demonstrate various forms of underspecification.

A lowercase x thus corresponds to a variable. By analogy with this extension, we also use a lowercase t instead of the normal ISO date–time separator of T to indicate that the time may need further specification: consider the third and fourth examples in Table 1, where it is not clear whether the time specified is a.m. or p.m.

For partially-specified dates and times, the string-based encoding thus both captures the local semantic content of the temporal expression, and provides a specification of what information the interpretation process has to add. If the temporal focus is encoded in the same form of representation, then producing the final interpretation is often a simple process of merging the two structures, with the values already specified in the intermediate representation taking precedence over those in the representation of the temporal focus. Expressions involving references to named months require a decision as to whether to look for the next or previous instance of the month, typically determined by the tense of the major clause containing the reference.

[5]Note that this does not mean the same thing as the use of an uppercase X in the TIMEX2 guidelines: an uppercase X means effectively that no value can be determined. Of course, if no value can be found for a variable element during the interpretation process, then the corresponding lowercase x will be replaced by an uppercase X.

String	Representation
9 pm	xxxx-xx-xxT21
11:59 pm	xxxx-xx-xxT23:59
eleven in the morning	xxxx-xx-xxT11:00
ten minutes to 3	xxxx-xx-xxt02:50
15 minutes after the hour	xxxx-xx-xxtxx:15
the nineteenth	xxxx-xx-19
January 3	xxxx-01-03
November	xxxx-11
summer	xxxx-SU
'63	xx63
the '60s	xx6

Table 1: Underspecified Dates and Times

4.2 Representing Weekdays

In recognition that the year-based calendar and the week-based calendar are not aligned, our intermediate representation embodies a special case borrowed from the TIMEX2 notation for days of the week that require context for their specification. Consider example (6a), uttered on Friday 14th April 2006; the intermediate semantic representation is provided in example (6b), and the final interpretation is provided in example (6c).

(6) a. We left on *Tuesday*.

b. `T-VAL="D2"`

c. `VAL="2006-04-11"`

This is not as convenient as the ISO-like encoding, and requires special case handling in the interpreter; however, a more comprehensive single representation would require abandoning the ISO-like encoding and the benefits it brings, so we choose to use the two formats in concert.

String	Representation
today	+0000-00-00
tomorrow	+0000-00-01
yesterday	−0000-00-01
five days ago	−0000-00-05
last month	−0000-01
last summer	−0001-SU
two weeks ago	−0000-W02
this weekend	+0000-W00-WE
this year	+0000
three years ago	−0003
the next century	+01

Table 2: Relative dates in ISO-like format.

The same notation supports references to parts of specific days, as presented in example (7).

(7) a. We left on *Tuesday morning.*
 b. `T-VAL="D2TMO"`
 c. `VAL="2006-04-11TMO"`

4.3 Relative Dates and Times

A relative date or time reference is one that requires a calendar arithmetic operation to be carried out with respect to some temporal focus in the text. Typical examples are as follows:

(8) a. We'll see him *tomorrow.*
 b. We saw him *last year.*
 c. We'll see him *next Thursday.*
 d. We saw him *last November.*

We distinguish three subtypes here: relative dates and times whose local semantics can be expressed in an ISO-like format; relative references to days and months by name; and less specific references to past, present and future times.

For the first of these, we extend the ISO format with a preceding '+' or '−' to indicate the direction from the current temporal focus. Some examples of dates are provided in Table 2, and some examples of date–time combinations are provided in Table 3. Note the both the date and time elements in a relative reference can be independently either absolute or relative: compare the representations for *in six hours time* and *at 6am today.*

This representation leads to a very intuitive coordinate-based arithmetic for computing the final semantic interpretation of a given expression: the interpreter merely adds the temporal focus and the intermediate value element-by-element from the smallest unit upwards, using carry arithmetic where appropriate.

String	Representation
sixty seconds later	+0000-00-00T+00:00:60
five minutes ago	+0000-00-00T−00:05
in six hours time	+0000-00-00T+06:00
at 6 a.m. today	+0000-00-00T06:00
last night	−0000-00-01TNI

Table 3: Relative times in ISO-like format.

String	Representation
last Monday	<D1
next Wednesday	>D3
last March	<M03
next March	>M03

Table 4: Relative References to Days and Months

Relative references to named days and months require a different treatment, in line with the notation introduced in Section 4.2. Table 4 shows the intermediate values used for a number of such expressions.

A further variation on this notation also allows us to specify a local semantics for expressions like *the first Tuesday* in temporal expressions like *the first Tuesday in July*, or like *the last year* in *the last year of the millenium*; see Table 5. To produce final interpretations of these, the interpreter has to construct the set of elements that correspond to the head noun (for example, a list of the ISO dates that correspond to the Tuesdays in a given month), and then select the nth element from that set.

5 Handling Embedded Constructions

The TIMEX specification allows for the embedding of one TIMEX within another. Consider an example like the following:

String	Representation
the first Tuesday	1D2
the second day	2D
the last Tuesday	$D2
the last day	$D

Table 5: Ordinally-specified Elements

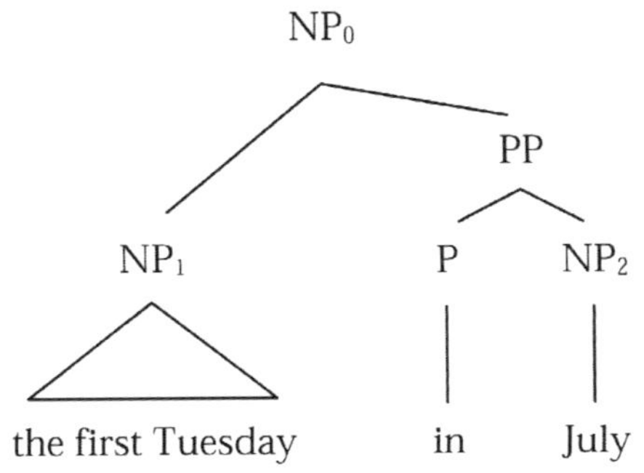

Figure 1: The syntactic structure of an embedded TIMEX

(9)
```
<TIMEX2>the first Tuesday
in<TIMEX2>July</TIMEX2></TIMEX2>
```

The bulk of the embedded TIMEXs provided as examples in the TIMEX guidelines are, like this one, of the form [NP PP], where the head NP contains a TIMEX, and the PP contains another TIMEX that is modified by the head NP. Syntactically, these structures are of the form shown in Figure 1.

For our purposes, it is convenient to first think of these structures as consisting of three, rather than two, TIMEXs, corresponding to the three subscripted NP nodes in this tree. The outermost TIMEX, corresponding to NP_0, is the one whose value we are ultimately interested in; this is computed by combining the semantics of the two constituent TIMEXs, corresponding to NP_1 and NP_2, and the preposition indicates how this combination should be carried out.

Structurally, the recognizer may first determine that there are two separate TIMEXs here:

(10)
```
<TIMEX2>the first
Tuesday</TIMEX2> in
<TIMEX2>July</TIMEX2>
```

Each of these TIMEXs can be given the appropriate local semantics by the recognizer; the recognizer then reorganizes this structure to mirror the embedding required by the TIMEX guidelines, to produce the structure shown in example (10) above; effectively, NP_1 disappears as a distinct constituent, and its intermediate semantics are inherited by NP_0.

We then leave it to the interpreter to combine the intermediate semantics of NP_0 with the intermediate semantics of NP_2 to produce a final semantics for NP_0: schematically, we have

(11) NP0(VAL) = NP0(T-VAL) $*$ NP2(T-VAL)

where '$*$' is the combinatory operation that corresponds to the preposition used. The operation required is specified by the recognizer as the value of the temporary attribute T-REL, which represents the semantics of the preposition.

The following three examples demonstrate a variety of possibilities, showing both the intermediate (T-VAL) and final (VAL) semantic interpretations in each case:

(12)
```
<TIMEX2 VAL="1999" T-VAL="$Y"
T-REL="OF">the last year of
<TIMEX2 VAL="1" T-VAL="+0">this
millennium</TIMEX2></TIMEX2>
```

(13)
```
<TIMEX2 VAL="1998-01-31"
T-VAL="$D" T-REL="OF">the last
day of <TIMEX2 VAL="1998-01"
T-VAL="xxxx-01">January
</TIMEX2></TIMEX2>
```

(14)
```
<TIMEX2 VAL="1998-01-31"
T-VAL="$D" T-REL="OF">the last
day of <TIMEX2 VAL="1998-01"
T-VAL="1998-01">January
1998</TIMEX2></TIMEX2>
```

Note that, when the embedded TIMEX is fully specified, as in the last example here, it would be possible for the recognizer to calculate the final value of the whole expression; however, for consistency we leave this task to the interpreter.

The semantics of the indicated T-REL depend on the types of its arguments. In the cases above, for example, the operation is one of selecting an ordinally-specified element of a list; but where the entity is a period rather than a point, as in *the first six months of 2005*, the operation is one of delimiting the period in question.

Of course, other forms of embedding are possible. In appositions, the syntactic structure can be thought of as [NP NP]; as in the case of embedded PPs, the TIMEX representation effectively promotes the semantics of the first NP to be the semantics of the whole. Again, we show both VAL and T-VAL values here, and the relevant T-REL.

(15)
```
<TIMEX2 VAL="1998-12-29"
T-VAL="xxxx-xx-xx"
```

```
T-REL="EQUAL">my birthday,
<TIMEX2 VAL="1998-12-29"
T-VAL="xxxx-12-29">December
twenty-ninth</TIMEX2></TIMEX2>
```

(16)
```
<TIMEX2 VAL="196" T-VAL="196"
T-REL="EQUAL">the 1960s, <TIMEX2
VAL="196" T-VAL="PXD">the days of
free love</TIMEX2></TIMEX2>
```

Here, the fact that the T-REL is EQUAL causes the interpreter to combine the values of the two TIMEXs, with points taking precedence over durations.

6 Conclusions

In this paper, we have argued that, in the context of interpreting temporal expressions, there is value in identifying a level of semantic representation that corresponds to the meaning of these expressions outside of any particular document context. This idea is not in itself new, and many existing systems appear to make use of such representations. However, we have proposed that this level of representation be made explicit; and by providing an encoding of this level of representation that is an extension of the existing TIMEX2 annotations in terms of element attributes and their values, we make it possible to assess the performance of systems with respect to intermediate values, final values, or both, using standard evaluation tools.

We have developed the representation described here on the basis of the set of 265 examples provided in the TIMEX2 guidelines (Ferro et al., 2005), and this set of annotated examples is available to the community.[6] The approach described here is implemented in DANTE, a text processing system which produces normalised values for all TIMEXs found in a document. The recognition component of the system, which constructs the intermediate representations described here, is implemented via just over 200 rules written in the JAPE language:[7] time expressions are thus recognised using finite state patterns, but we then apply a syntactic check, using the Connexor parser, to ensure that we have identified the full extent of each temporal expression, appropriately extending the extent when this is not the case.

[6]See www.clt.mq.edu.au/timex.

[7]JAPE is provided as part of the GATE tools (Cunningham et al., 2002).

We are currently testing this representation and its means of derivation against the data from the 2004 TERN competition. Our results are broadly comparable to those achieved by other systems (for example, Chronos or TempEx), though they can not be compared directly since the reported evaluations at the TERN competition use data which are not public and therefore not available to us.

7 Acknowledgements

We acknowledge the support of the Defence Science and Technology Organisation in carrying out the work described here.

References

H. Cunningham, D. Maynard, K. Bontcheva, and V. Tablan. 2002. GATE: A framework and graphical development environment for robust NLP tools and applications. In *Proceedings of the 40th Anniversary Meeting of the ACL.*

L. Ferro, L. Gerber, I. Mani, B. Sundheim, and G. Wilson. 2005. TIDES 2005 Standard for the Annotation of Temporal Expressions. Technical report, MITRE, September.

J. R. Hobbs and F. Pan. 2004. An ontology of time for the semantic web. *ACM Transactions on Asian Language Information Processing*, 3(1):66–85, March.

I. Mani, J. Pustejovsky, and R. Gaizauskas, editors. 2005. *The Language of Time*. Oxford Univ. Press.

M. Negri and L. Marseglia. 2005. Recognition and normalization of time expressions: ITC-IRST at TERN 2004. Technical Report WP3.7, Information Society Technologies, February.

I. Pratt and N. Francez. 2001. Temporal prepositions and temporal generalized quantifiers. *Linguistics and Philosophy*, 24:187–222.

J. Pustejovsky, J. Castaño, R. Ingria, R. Gaizauskas R. Saur, A. Setzer, and G. Katz. 2003. TimeML: Robust Specification of Event and Temporal Expressions in Text. In *IWCS-5, Fifth International Workshop on Computational Semantics.*

E. Saquete, P. Martínez-Barco, and R. Muñoz. 2002. Recognising and Tagging Temporal Expressions in Spanish. In *Proc. of LREC'02: Workshop on Annotation Standards for Temporal Information in Natural Language, Las Palmas, Spain.*

F. Schilder. 2004. Extracting meaning from temporal nouns and temporal prepositions. *ACM Transactions on Asian Language Information Processing*, 3(1):33–50, March.

Automatic Dating of Documents and Temporal Text Classification

Angelo Dalli
NLP Research Group
University of Sheffield
United Kingdom
angelo@dcs.shef.ac.uk

Yorick Wilks
NLP Research Group
University of Sheffield
United Kingdom
yorick@dcs.shef.ac.uk

Abstract

The frequency of occurrence of words in natural languages exhibits a periodic and a non-periodic component when analysed as a time series. This work presents an unsupervised method of extracting periodicity information from text, enabling time series creation and filtering to be used in the creation of sophisticated language models that can discern between repetitive trends and non-repetitive writing patterns. The algorithm performs in $O(n \log n)$ time for input of length n. The temporal language model is used to create rules based on temporal-word associations inferred from the time series. The rules are used to guess automatically at likely document creation dates, based on the assumption that natural languages have unique signatures of changing word distributions over time. Experimental results on news items spanning a nine year period show that the proposed method and algorithms are accurate in discovering periodicity patterns and in dating documents automatically solely from their content.

1 Introduction

Various features have been used to classify and predict the characteristics of text and related text documents, ranging from simple word count models to sophisticated clustering and Bayesian models that can handle both linear and non-linear classes. The general goal of most classification research is to assign objects from a pre-defined domain (such as words or entire documents) to two or more classes/categories. Current and past research has largely focused on solving problems like tagging, sense disambiguation, sentiment classification, author and language identification and topic classification. In this paper, we introduce an unsupervised method that classifies text and documents according to their predicted time of writing/creation. The method uses a sophisticated temporal language model to predict likely creation dates for a document, hence dating it automatically.

This paper presents the main assumption behind this work together some background information about existing techniques and the implemented system, followed by a brief explanation of the classification and dating method, and finally concluding with results and evaluation performed on the LDC GigaWord English Corpus (LDC, 2003) together with its implications and relevance to temporal-analytical frameworks and TimeML applications.

2 Background and Assumptions

The main assumption behind this work is that natural language exhibits a unique signature of varying word frequencies over time. New words come into popular use continually, while other words fall into disuse either after a brief fad or when they become obsolete or archaic. Current events, popular issues and topics also affect writers in their choice of words and so does the time period when they create documents. This assumption is implicitly made when people try to guess at the creation date of a document – we would expect a document written in Shakespeare's time to contain higher frequency counts of words and phrases such as "thou art", "betwixt", "fain", "methinks", "vouchsafe" and so on than would a modern 21st century document. Similarly, a document that contains a high frequency of occurrence of the words "terrorism", "Al Qaeda", "World Trade Center", and so on is more likely to be written after 11 September 2001. New words can also be used to create absolute constraints on the creation dates of documents, for example, it is highly improbable that a

Proceedings of the Workshop on Annotating and Reasoning about Time and Events, pages 17–22,
Sydney, July 2006. ©2006 Association for Computational Linguistics

document containing the word "blog" was written before July 1999 (it was first used in a newsgroup in July 1999 as an abbreviation for "weblog"), or a document containing the word "Google" to have been written before 1997. Words that are now in common use can also be used to impose constraints on the creation date; for example, the word "bedazzled" has been attributed to Shakespeare, thus allowing documents from his time onwards to be identifiable automatically. Traditional dictionaries often try to record the date of appearance of new words in the language and there are various Internet sites, such as WordSpy.com, devoted to chronicling the appearance of new words and their meanings. Our system is building up a knowledge base of the first occurrences of various words in different languages, enabling more accurate constraints to be imposed on the likely document creation date automatically.

Commercial trademarks and company names are also useful in dating documents, as their registration date is usually available in public registries. Temporal information extracted from the documents itself is also useful in dating the documents – for example, if a document contains many references to the year 2006, it is quite likely that the document was written in 2006 (or in the last few weeks of December 2005).

These notions have been used implicitly by researchers and historians when validating the authenticity of documents, but have not been utilised much in automated systems. Similar applications have so far been largely confined to authorship identification, such as (Mosteller and Wallace, 1964; Fung, 2003) and the identification of association rules (Yarowsky, 1994; Silverstein et al., 1997).

Temporal information is presently underutilised for automated document classification purposes, especially when it comes to guessing at the document creation date automatically. This work presents a method of using periodical temporal-frequency information present in documents to create temporal-association rules that can be used for automatic document dating.

Past and ongoing related research work has largely focused on the identification and tagging of temporal expressions, with the creation of tagging methodologies such as TimeML/TIMEX (Gaizauskas and Setzer, 2002; Pustejovsky et al., 2003; Ferro et al., 2004), TDRL (Aramburu and Berlanga, 1998) and their associated evaluations such as the ACE TERN competition (Sundheim et al. 2004).

Temporal analysis has also been applied in Question-Answering systems (Pustejovsky et al., 2004; Schilder and Habel, 2003; Prager et al., 2003), email classification (Kiritchenko et al., 2004), aiding the precision of Information Retrieval results (Berlanga et al., 2001), document summarisation (Mani and Wilson, 2000), time stamping of event clauses (Filatova and Hovy, 2001), temporal ordering of events (Mani et al., 2003) and temporal reasoning from text (Boguraev and Ando, 2005; Moldovan et al., 2005).

A growing body of related work related to the computational treatment of time in language has also been building up largely since 2000 (COLING 2000; ACL 2001; LREC 2002; TERQAS 2002; TANGO 2003, Dagstuhl 2005).

There is also a large body of work on time series analysis and temporal logic in Physics, Economics and Mathematics, providing important techniques and general background information. In particular, this work uses techniques adapted from Seasonal ARIMA (auto-regressive integrated moving average) models (SARIMA). SARIMA models are a class of seasonal, non-stationary temporal models based on the ARIMA process. The ARIMA process is further defined as a non-stationary extension of the stationary ARMA model. The ARMA model is one of the most widely used models when analyzing time series, especially in Physics, and incorporate both auto-regressive terms and moving average terms (Box and Jenkins, 1976). Non-stationary ARIMA processes are defined by the following equation:

$$(1-B)^d \phi(B) X_t = \theta(B) Z_t \qquad (1)$$

where d is non-negative integer, and $\phi(X)$ $\theta(X)$ polynomials of degrees p and q respectively. The SARIMA extension adds seasonal AR and MA polynomials that can handle seasonally varying data in time series.

The exact formulation of the SARIMA model is beyond the scope of this paper and can be found in various mathematics and physics publications, such as (Chatfield, 2003; Brockwell et al., 1991; Janacek, 2001).

The main drawback of SARIMA modelling (and associated models built on the basic ARMA model) is that it requires fairly long time series before accurate results are obtained. The majority of authors recommend that a time series of at least 50 data points is used to build the SARIMA model.

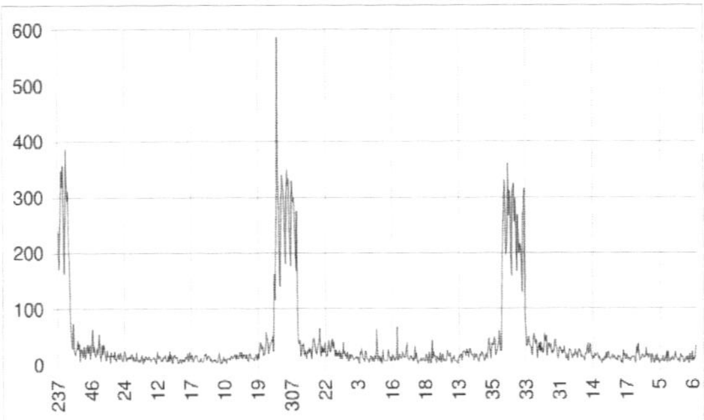

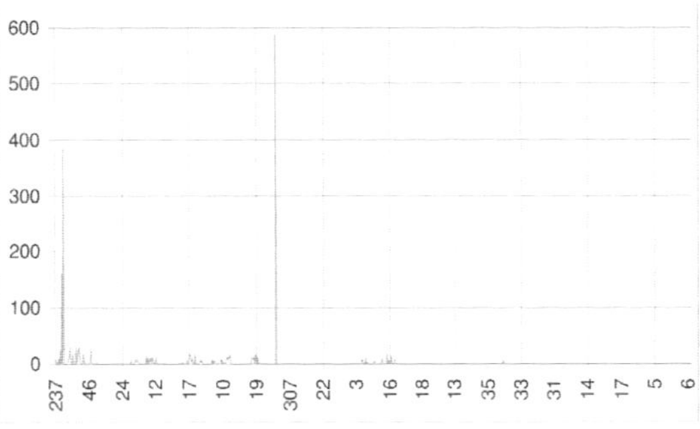

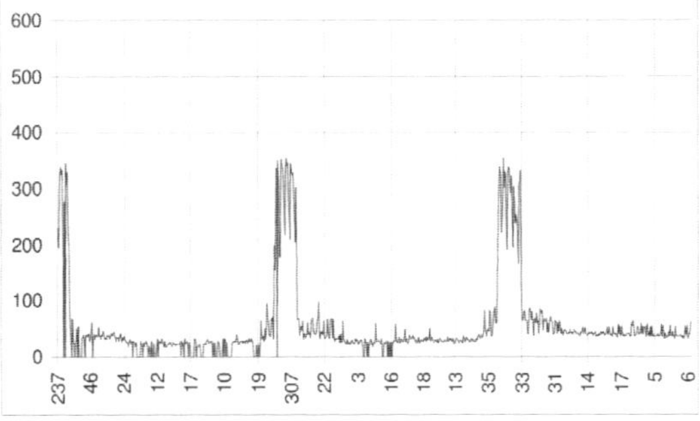

Time Series for "January"
Original (Top Left), Non-Periodic Component (Top Right), Periodic Component (Bottom Right)

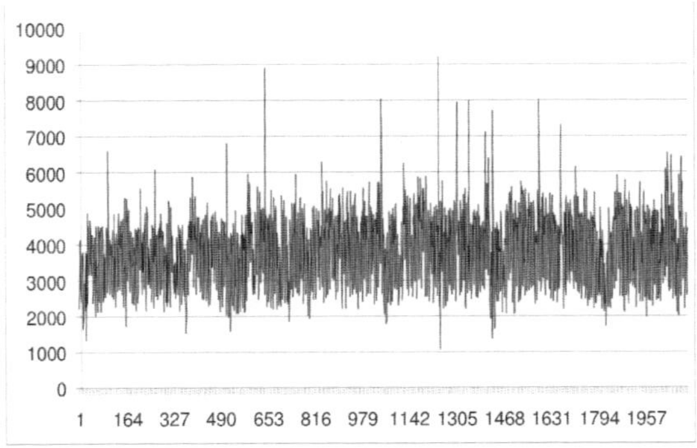

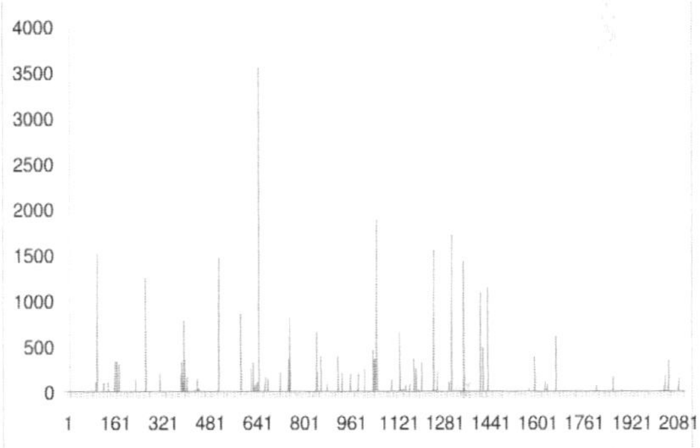

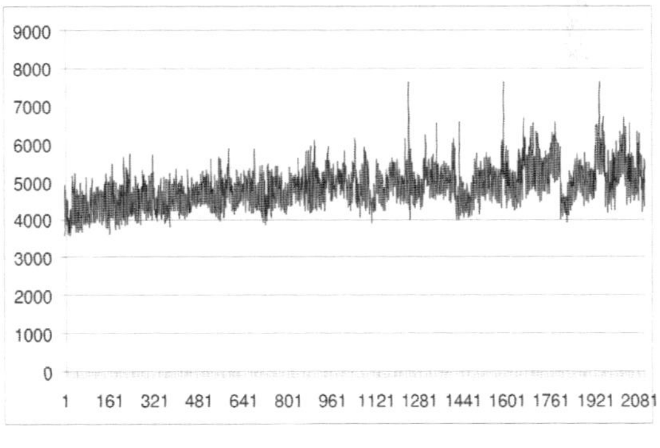

Time Series for "The"
Original (Top Left), Non-Periodic Component (Top Right), Periodic Component (Bottom Right)

Figure 1: Effects of applying the temporal periodical algorithm on time series for "January" (top three graphs) and "the" (bottom three graphs) with the original series on the left and the remaining time series components after filtering on the right. Y-axis shows frequency count and X-axis shows the day number (time).

3 Temporal Periodicity Analysis

We have created a high-performance system that decomposes time series into two parts: a periodic component that repeats itself in a predictable manner, and a non-periodic component that is left after the periodic component has been filtered out from the original time series. Figure 1 shows an example of the filtering results on time-series of the words "January" and "the". The original series is presented together with two series representing the periodic and non-periodic components of the original time series. The time series are based on training documents selected at random from the GigaWord English corpus. 10% of all the documents in the corpus were used as training documents, with the rest being available for evaluation and testing. A total of 395,944 time series spanning 9 years were calculated from the GigaWord corpus. The availability of 9 years of data also mitigated the negative effects of using short time series in combination with SARIMA models (as up to 3,287 data points were available for some words, well above the 50 data point minimum recommendation). Figure 2 presents pseudo-code for the time series decomposition algorithm:

```
1. Find min/max/mean and standard deviation of time series
2. Start with a pre-defined maximum window size (set to 366 days in our present system)
3. While window size bigger than 1 repeat steps a. to d. below:
     a. Look at current value in time series (starting from first value)
     b. Do values at positions current, current + window size, current + 2 x window size, etc. vary by less than half a standard deviation?
     c. If yes, mark current value/window size pair as being possible decomposition match
     d. Look at next value in time series until the end is reached
     e. Decrease window size by one
4. Select the minimum number of decomposition matches that cover the entire time series using a greedy algorithm
```

Figure 2: Time Series Decomposition Algorithm

The time series decomposition algorithm was applied to the 395,944 time series, taking an average of 419ms per series. The algorithm runs in $O(n \log n)$ time for a time series of length n.

The periodic component of the time series is then analysed to extract temporal association rules between words and different "seasons", including Day of Week, Week Number, Month Number, Quarter, and Year. The procedure of determining if a word, for example, is predominantly peaking on a weekly basis, is to apply a sliding window of size 7 (in the case of weekly periods) and determining if the periodic time series always spikes within this window. Figure 3 shows the frequency distribution of the periodic time series component of the days of week names ("Monday", "Tuesday", etc.) Note that the frequency counts peak exactly on that particular day of the week. Thus, for example, the word "Monday" is automatically associated with Day 1, and "April" associated with Month 4.

The creation of temporal association rules generalises the inferences obtained from the periodic data. Each association rule has the following information:

- Word ID
- Period Type (Week, Month, etc.)
- Period Number and Score Matrix

The period number and score matrix represent a probability density function that shows the likelihood of a word appearing on a particular period number. Thus, for example, the score matrix for "January" will have a high score for period 1 (and period type set to Monthly). Figure 4 shows some examples of extracted association rules. The probability density function (PDF) scores are shown in Figure 4 as they are stored internally (as multiples of the standard deviation of that time series) and are automatically normalised during the classification process at runtime. The standard deviation of values in the time series is used instead of absolute values in order to reduce the variance between fluctuations in different time series for words that occur frequently (like pronouns) and those that appear relatively less frequently.

Rule generalisation is not possible in such a straightforward manner for the non-periodic data. In this paper, the use of non-periodic data to optimise the results of the temporal classification and automatic dating system is not covered. Non-periodic data may be used to generate specific rules that are associated only with particular dates or date ranges. Non-periodic data can also use information obtained from hapax words and other low-frequency words to generate additional refinement rules. However, there is a danger that relying on rules extracted from non-periodic data will simply reflect the specific characteristics of the corpus used to train the system, rather than the language in general. Ongoing research is being performed into calculating relevance levels for rules extracted from non-periodic data.

4 Temporal Classification and Automatic Dating

The periodic temporal association rules are utilised to guess automatically the creation date of documents. Documents are input into the system and the probability density functions for each word are weighted and added up. Each PDF is weighted according to the inverse document frequency (idf) of each associated word. Periods that obtain high score are then ranked for each type of period and two guesses per period type are obtained for each document. Ten guesses in total are thus obtained for Day of Week, Week Number, Month Number, Quarter, and Year (5 period types x 2 guesses each).

	Su	M	T	W	Th	F	S
0	**22660**	10540	7557	772	2130	3264	11672
1	12461	**37522**	10335	6599	1649	3222	3414
2	3394	18289	**38320**	9352	7300	2543	2261
3	2668	4119	18120	**36933**	10427	5762	2147
4	2052	2602	3910	17492	**36094**	9098	5667
5	5742	1889	2481	2568	17002	**32597**	7849
6	7994	7072	1924	1428	3050	14087	**21468**
Av	8138	11719	11806	10734	11093	10081	7782
St	7357	12711	12974	12933	12308	10746	6930

Figure 3: Days of Week Temporal Frequency Distribution for extracted Periodic Component displayed in a Weekly Period Type format

January

Week	*1*	*2*	*3*	*4*	*5*
Score	1.48	2.20	3.60	3.43	3.52

Month *1* Score 2.95
Quarter *1* Score 1.50

Christmas

Week	*2*	*5*	*36*	*42*	*44*
Score	1.32	0.73	1.60	0.83	1.32
Week	*47*	*49*	*50*	*51*	*52*
Score	1.32	2.20	2.52	2.13	1.16

Month	*1*	*9*	*10*	*11*	*12*
Score	1.10	0.75	1.63	1.73	1.98

Quarter *4* Score 1.07

Figure 4: Temporal Classification Rules for Periodic Components of "January" and "Christmas"

4.1 TimeML Output

The system can output TimeML compliant markup tags using TIMEX that can be used by other TimeML compliant applications especially during temporal normalization processes. If the base anchor reference date for a document is unknown, and a document contains relative temporal references exclusively, our system output can provide a baseline date that can be used to normalize all the relative dates mentioned in the document. The system has been integrated with a fine-grained temporal analysis system based on TimeML, with promising results, especially when processing documents obtained from the Internet.

5 Evaluation, Results and Conclusion

The system was trained using 67,000 news items selected at random from the GigaWord corpus. The evaluation took place on 678,924 news items extracted from items marked as being of type "story" or "multi" in the GigaWord corpus. Table 1 presents a summary of the evaluation results. Processing took around 2.33ms per item.

The actual date was extracted from each news item in the GigaWord corpus and the day of week (DOW), week number and quarter calculated from the actual date.

This information was then used to evaluate the system performance automatically. The average error for each type of classifier was also calculated automatically. For a result to be considered as correct, the system had to have the predicted value ranked in the first position equal to the actual value (of the type of period).

Type	Correct	Incorrect	Avg. Error
DOW	218,899 (32.24%)	460,025 (67.75%)	1.89 days
Week	24,660 (3.53%)	654,264 (96.36%)	14.37 wks
Month	122,777 (18.08%)	556,147 (81.91%)	2.57 mths
Quarter	337,384 (49.69%)	341,540 (50.30%)	1.48 qts
Year	596,009 (87.78%)	82,915 (12.21%)	1.74 yrs

Table 1: Evaluation Results Summary

The system results show that reasonable accurate dates can be guessed at the quarterly and yearly levels. The weekly classifier had the worst performance of all classifiers, likely as a result of weak association between periodical word frequencies and week numbers. Logical/sanity checks can be performed on ambiguous results. For example, consider a document written on 4 January 2006 and that the periodical classifiers give the following results for this particular document:

- DOW = Wednesday
- Week = 52
- Month = January

- Quarter = 1
- Year = 2006

These results are typical of the system, as particular classifiers sometimes get the period incorrect. In this example, the weekly classifier incorrectly classified the document as pertaining to week 52 (at the end of the year) instead of the beginning of the year. The system will use the facts that the monthly and quarterly classifiers agree together with the fact that week 1 follows week 52 if seen as a continuous cycle of weeks to correctly classify the document as being created on a Wednesday in January 2006.

The capability to automatically date texts and documents solely from its contents (without any additional external clues or hints) is undoubtedly useful in various contexts, such as the forensic analysis of undated instant messages or emails (where the Day of Week classifier can be used to create partial orderings), and in authorship identification studies (where the Year classifier can be used to check that the text pertains to an acceptable range of years).

The temporal classification and analysis system presented in this paper can handle any Indo-European language in its present form. Further work is being carried out to extend the system to Chinese and Arabic. Evaluations will be carried out on the GigaWord Chinese and GigaWord Arabic corpora for consistency. Current research is aiming at improving the accuracy of the classifier by using the non-periodic components and integrating a combined classification method with other systems.

References

Aramburu, M. Berlanga, R. 1998. *A Retrieval Language for Historical Documents*. Springer Verlag LNCS, 1460, pp. 216-225.

Berlanga, R. Perez, J. Aramburu, M. Llido, D. 2001. *Techniques and Tools for the Temporal Analysis of Retrieved Information*. Springer Verlag LNCS, 2113, pp. 72-81.

Boguraev, B. Ando, R.K. 2005. *TimeML-Compliant Text Analysis for Temporal Reasoning*. IJCAI-2005, pp. 997-1003.

Box, G. Jenkins, G. 1976. *Time Series Analysis: Forecasting and Control*, Holden-Day.

Brockwell, P.J. Fienberg, S. Davis, R. 1991. *Time Series: Theory and Methods*. Springer-Verlag.

Chatfield, C. 2003. *The Analysis of Time Series*. CRC Press.

Ferro, L. Gerber, L. Mani, I. Sundheim, B. Wilson, G. 2004. *TIDES Standard for the Annotation of Temporal Expressions*. The MITRE Corporation.

Filatova, E. Hovy, E. 2001. *Assigning time-stamps to event-clauses*. Proc. EACL 2001, Toulouse.

Fung, G. 2003. *The Disputed Federalist Papers: SVM Feature Selection via Concave Minimization*. New York City, ACM Press.

Gaizauskas, R. Setzer, A. 2002. *Annotation Standards for Temporal Information in NL*. LREC 2002.

Janacek, G. 2001. *Practical Time Series*. Oxford U.P.

Kiritchenko, S. Matwin, S. Abu-Hakima, S. 2004. *Email Classification with Temporal Features*. Proc. IIPWM 2004, Zakopane, Poland. Springer Verlag Advances in Soft Computing, pp. 523-534.

Linguistic Data Consortium (LDC). 2003. English Gigaword Corpus. David Graff, ed. LDC2003T05.

Mani, I. Wilson, G. 2000. *Robust temporal processing of news*. Proc. ACL 2000, Hong Kong.

Mani, I. Schiffman, B. Zhang, J. 2003. *Inferring temporal ordering of events in news*. Proc. HLT-NAACL 2003, Edmonton, Canada.

Moldovan, D. Clark, C. Harabagiu, S. 2005. *Temporal Context Representation and Reasoning*. IJCAI-2005, pp. 1099-1104.

Mosteller, F. Wallace, D. 1964. *Inference and Disputed Authorship: Federalist.* Addison-Wesley.

Prager, J. Chu-Carroll, J. Brown, E. Czuba, C. 2003. *Question Answering using predictive annotation*. In Advances in Question Answering, Hong Kong.

Pustejovsky, J. Castano, R. Ingria, R. Sauri, R. Gaizauskas, R. Setzer, A. Katz, G. 2003. *TimeML: Robust Specification of event and temporal expressions in text*. IWCS-5.

Pustejovsky, J. Sauri, R. Castano, J. Radev, D. Gaizauskas, R. Setzer, A. Sundheim, B. Katz, G. 2004. "Representing Temporal and Event Knowledge for QA Systems". *New Directions in QA*, MIT Press.

Schilder, F. Habel, C. 2003. *Temporal Information Extraction for Temporal QA*. AAAI Spring Symp., Stanford, CA. pp. 35-44.

Silverstein, C. Brin, S. Motwani, R. 1997. *Beyond Market Baskets: Generalizing Association Rules to Dependence Rules*. Data Mining and Knowledge Discovery.

Sundheim, B. Gerber, L. Ferro, L. Mani, I. Wilson, G. 2004. *Time Expression Recognition and Normalization (TERN)*. MITRE, Northrop Grumman, SPAWAR. http://timex2.mitre.org.

Yarowsky, D. 1994. Decision Lists For Lexical Ambiguity Resolution: Application to Accent Restoration in Spanish and French. ACL 1994.

A Pilot Study on Acquiring Metric Temporal Constraints for Events

Inderjeet Mani and Ben Wellner
The MITRE Corporation
202 Burlington Road, Bedford, MA 01730, USA
and
Department of Computer Science, Brandeis University
415 South St., Waltham, MA 02254, USA
{imani, wellner}@mitre.org

Abstract

Previous research on temporal anchoring and ordering has focused on the annotation and learning of temporal relations between events. These qualitative relations can be usefully supplemented with information about metric constraints, specifically as to how long events last. This paper describes the first steps in acquiring metric temporal constraints for events. The work is carried out in the context of the TimeML framework for marking up events and their temporal relations. This pilot study examines the feasibility of acquisition of metric temporal constraints from corpora.

1 Introduction

The growing interest in practical NLP applications such as question-answering and text summarization places increasing demands on the processing of temporal information. In multi-document summarization of news articles, it can be useful to know the relative order of events so as to merge and present information from multiple news sources correctly. In question-answering, one would like to be able to ask when an event occurs, or what events occurred prior to a particular event. A wealth of prior research by (Passoneau 1988), (Webber 1988), (Hwang and Schubert 1992), (Kamp and Reyle 1993), (Lascarides and Asher 1993), (Hitzeman et al. 1995), (Kehler 2000) and others, has explored the different knowledge sources used in inferring the temporal ordering of events, including temporal adverbials, tense, aspect, rhetorical relations, pragmatic conventions, and background knowledge. For example, the narrative convention of events being described in the order in which they occur is followed in (1), but overridden by means of a discourse relation, Explanation in (2).

```
(1) Max stood up. John greeted him.
(2) Max fell. John pushed him.
```

While there has been a spurt of recent research addressing the event ordering problem, e.g., (Mani and Wilson 2000) (Filatova and Hovy 2001) (Schilder and Habel 2001) (Li et al. 2001) (Mani et al. 2003) (Li et al. 2004) (Lapata and Lascarides 2004) (Boguraev and Ando 2005) (Mani et al. 2006), that research relies on qualitative temporal relations. Qualitative relations (e.g., event A BEFORE event B, or event A DURING time T) are certainly of interest in developing timelines of events in news and other genres. However, metric constraints can also be potentially useful in this ordering problem. For example, in (3), it can be crucial to know whether the bomb landed a few minutes to hours or several years BEFORE the hospitalization. While humans have strong intuitions about this from commonsense knowledge, machines don't.

(3) An elderly Catholic man was *hospitalized* from cuts after a Protestant gasoline bomb *landed* in his back yard.

Fortunately, there are numerous instances such as (4), where metric constraints are specified explicitly:

(4) The company *announced* <u>Tuesday</u> that <u>third quarter</u> sales *had fallen*.

In (4), the falling of sales occurred over the three-month period of time inferable from the speech time. However, while the announcement is anchored to a day inferable from the speech

Proceedings of the Workshop on Annotating and Reasoning about Time and Events, pages 23–29,
Sydney, July 2006. ©2006 Association for Computational Linguistics

time, the length of the announcement is not specified.

These examples suggest that it may be possible to mine information from a corpus to fill in extents for the time intervals of and between events, when these are either unspecified or partially specified. Metric constraints can also potentially lead to better qualitative links, e.g., events with long durations are more likely to overlap with other events.

This paper describes some preliminary experiments to acquire metric constraints. The approach extends the TimeML representation (Pustejovsky et al. 2005) to include such constraints. We first translate a TimeML representation with qualitative relations into one where metric constraints are added. This representation may tell us how long certain events last, and the length of the gaps between them, given the information in the text. However, the information in the text may be incomplete; some extents may be unknown. We therefore need an external source of knowledge regarding the typical extents of events, which we can use when the text doesn't provide it. We accordingly describe an initial attempt to bootstrap event durations from raw corpora as well as corpora annotated with qualitative relations.

2 Annotation Scheme and Corpora

TimeML (Pustejovsky et al. 2005) (www.timeml.org) is an annotation scheme for markup of events, times, and their qualitative temporal relations in news articles. The TimeML scheme flags tensed verbs, adjectives, and nominals with EVENT tags with various attributes, including the class of event, tense, grammatical aspect, polarity (negative or positive), any modal operators which govern the event being tagged, and cardinality of the event if it's mentioned more than once. Likewise, time expressions are flagged and their values normalized, based on an extension of the ACE (2004) (tern.mitre.org) TIMEX2 annotation scheme (called TIMEX3).

For temporal relations, TimeML defines a TLINK tag that links tagged events to other events and/or times. For example, given sentence (4), a TLINK tag will **anchor** the event instance of announcing to the time expression *Tuesday* (whose normalized value will be inferred from context), with the relation IS_INCLUDED. This is shown in (5).

```
(5) The company <EVENT even-
tID=e1>announced</EVENT> <TIMEX3
tid=t1 value=1998-01-08>Tuesday
</TIMEX3> that <TIMEX3 tid=t2
value=P1Q3 beginPoint=t3 end-
Point=t4>third-quarter</TIMEX3>
sales <EVENT eventID=e2> had
fallen</EVENT>.
<TLINK eventID=e1 relatedToEven-
tID=e2 relType=AFTER/>
<TLINK eventID=e1 relatedToTimeID=t1
relType=IS_INCLUDED/>
<TIMEX3 tid=t3 value=1997-07/>
<TIMEX3 tid=t4 value=1997-09/>
```

The representation of time expressions in TimeML uses TIMEX2, which is an extension of the TIMEX2 scheme (Ferro et al. 2005). It represents three different kinds of time values: points in time (answering the question "when?"), durations (answering "how long?"), and frequencies (answering "how often?")[1].

TimeML uses 14 temporal relations in the TLINK relTypes. Among these, the 6 inverse relations are redundant. In order to have a non-hierarchical classification, SIMULTANEOUS and IDENTITY are collapsed, since IDENTITY is a subtype of SIMULTANEOUS. (An event or time is SIMULTANEOUS with another event or time if they occupy the same time interval. X and Y are IDENTICAL if they are simultaneous *and* coreferential). DURING and IS_INCLUDED are collapsed since DURING is a subtype of IS_INCLUDED that anchors events to times that are durations. (An event or time INCLUDES another event or time if the latter occupies a proper subinterval of the former.) IBEFORE (immediately before) corresponds to MEETS in Allen's interval calculus (Allen 1984). Allen's OVERLAPS relation is not represented in TimeML.

The above considerations allow us to collapse the TLINK relations to a disjunctive classification of 6 temporal relations *TRels* = {SIMULTANEOUS, IBEFORE, BEFORE, BEGINS, ENDS, INCLUDES}. These 6 relations and their inverses map one-to-one to 12 of Allen's 13 basic relations (Allen 1984).

Formally, each TLINK is a constraint of the general form x R y, where x and y are intervals, and R is a disjunct $\vee_{i=1,..,6}(r_i)$, where r_i is a relation in *TRels*. In annotating a document for Ti-

[1] Our representation (using t3 and t4) grounds the fuzzy primitive P1Q3 (i.e., a period of one 3rd-quarter) to specific months, though this is an application-specific step. In analyzing our data, we normalize P1Q3 as P3M (i.e., a period of 3 months). For conciseness, we omit TimeML EVENT and TIMEX3 attributes that aren't relevant to the discussion.

meML, the annotator adds a TLINK iff she can commit to the TLINK relType being unambiguous, i.e., having exactly one relType r.

Two human-annotated corpora have been released based on TimeML[2]: TimeBank 1.2 (Pustejovsky et al. 2003) with 186 documents and 64,077 words of text, and the Opinion Corpus (www.timeml.org), with 73 documents and 38,709 words. TimeBank 1.2 (we use 1.2.a) was created in the early stages of TimeML development, and was partitioned across five annotators with different levels of expertise. The Opinion Corpus was developed recently, and was partitioned across just two highly trained annotators, and could therefore be expected to be less noisy. In our experiments, we merged the two datasets to produce a single corpus, called OTC.

3 Translation

3.1 Introduction

The first step is to translate a TimeML representation with qualitative relations into one where metric constraints are added. This translation needs to produce a consistent metric representation. The temporal extents of events, and between events, can be read off, when there are no unknowns, from the metric representation. The problem, however is that the representation may have unknowns, and the extents may not be minimal.

3.2 Mapping to Metric Representation

Let each event or time interval x be represented as a pair of start and end time points <x1, x2>. For example, given sentence (4), and the TimeML representation shown in (5), let x be *fall* and y be *announce*. Then, we have x1 = 19970701T00, x2 = 19970930T23:59, y1 = 19980108Tn1, y2 = 19980108Tn2 (here T represents time of day in hours).

To add metric constraints, given a pair of events or times x and y, where x=<x1, x2> and y=<y1, y2>, we need to add, based on the qualitative relation between x and y, constraints of the general form (xi-yj) $\leq$ n, for $1 \leq i, j \leq 2$. We follow precisely the method 'Allen-to-metric' of (Kautz and Ladkin 1991) which defines metric constraints for each relation R in *TRels*. For example, here is a qualitative relation and its metric constraints:

```
(6) x is BEFORE y iff (x2-y1) < 0.
```

[2]More details can be found at timeml.org.

In our example, where x is *fall* and y is the *announce*, we are given the qualitative relationship that x is BEFORE Y, so the metric constraint (x2-y1) < 0 can be asserted.

Consider another qualitative relation and its metric constraint:

```
(7) z INCLUDES y iff (z1-y1) < 0 and
(y2-z2) < 0.
```

Let y be *announce* in (4), as before, and let z=<z1, z2> be the time of *Tuesday*, where z1 = 19980108T00, and z2 = 19980108T23:59. Since we are given the qualitative relation y IS_INCLUDED z, the metric constraints (z1-y1) < 0 and (y2-z2) < 0 can be asserted.

3.3 Consistency Checking

We now turn to the general problem of checking consistency. The set of TLINKs for a document constitutes a graph, where the nodes are events or times, and the edges are TLINKs. Given such a TimeML-derived graph for a document, a temporal closure algorithm (Verhagen 2005) carries out a transitive closure of the graph. The transitive closure algorithm was inspired by (Setzer and Gaizauskas 2000) and is based on Allen's interval algebra, taking into account the limitations on that algebra that were pointed out by (Vilain et al. 1990). It is basically a constraint propagation algorithm that uses a transitivity table to model the compositional behavior of all pairs of relations in a document. The algorithm's transitivity table is represented by 745 axioms. An example axiom is shown in (8):

```
(8) If relation(A, B) = BEFORE &&
   relation(B, C) = INCLUDES
then infer relation(A, C) = BEFORE.
```

In propagating constraints, links added by closure can have a disjunction of one or more relations in *TRels*. When the algorithm terminates, any TLINK with more than one disjunct is discarded. Thus, a closed graph is consistent and has a single relType r in *TRels* for each TLINK edge. The algorithm runs in $O(n^3)$ time, where n is the number of intervals.

The closed graph is augmented so that whenever input edges a r_1 b and b r_2 c are composed to yield the output edge a r_3 c, where r1, r2, and r3 are in *TRels*, the metric constraints for r_3 are added to the output edge. To continue our example, since the *fall* x is BEFORE the Tuesday z and z INCLUDES y (*announce*), we can infer, using rule 8, that x is BEFORE y, i.e., that *fall* precedes *announce*. Using rule (6), we can again assert that (x2-y1) < 0.

3.4 Reading off Temporal Extents

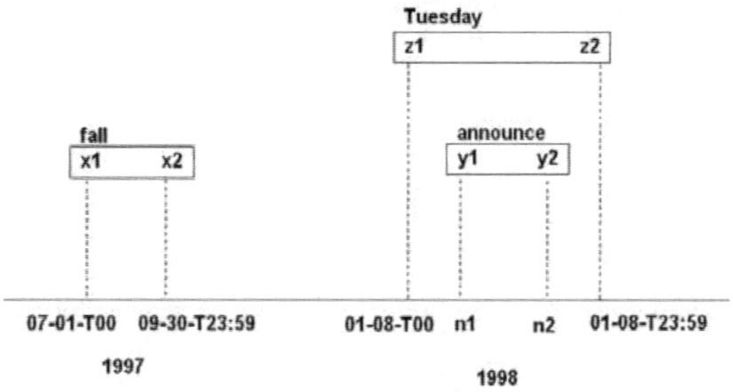

Figure 1. Metric Constraints

We now have the metric constraints added to the graph in a consistent manner. It remains to compute, given each event or time x=<x1, x2>, the values for x1 and x2. In our example, we have *fall* x=<19970701T00, 19970930T23:59>, *announce* y=<19980108Tn1, 19980108Tn2>, and <u>Tuesday</u> z=<19980108T00, 19980108T23:59>, and the added metric constraints that (x2-y1), (z1-y1), and (y2-z2) are all negative. Graphically, this can be pictured as in Figure 1.

As can be see in Figure 1, there are still unknowns (n1 and n2): we aren't told exactly how long *announce* lasted -- it could be anywhere up to a day. We therefore need to acquire information about how long events last when the example text doesn't tell us. We now turn to this problem.

4 Acquisition

We started with the 4593 event-time TLINKs we found in the unclosed human-annotated OTC. From these, we restricted ourselves to those where the times involved were of type TIMEX3 DURATION. We augmented the TimeBank data with information from the raw (un-annotated) British National Corpus. We tried a variety of search patterns to try and elicit durations, finally converging on the single pattern "lasted". There were 1325 hits for this query in the BNC. (The public web interface to the BNC only shows 50 random results at a time, so we had to iterate.) The retrieved hits (sentences and fragments of sentences) were then processed with components from the TARSQI toolkit (Verhagen et al. 2005) to provide automatic TimeML annotations. The TLINKs between events and times that were TIMEX3 DURATIONS were then extracted. These links were then corrected and validated by hand and then added to the OTC data to form an integrated corpus. An example from the BNC is shown in (9).

```
(9)     The     <EVENT>storm</EVENT>
<EVENT>lasted</EVENT>          <TIMEX3
VAL="P5D">five days</TIMEX3>.
```

Next, the resulting data was subject to morphological normalization in a semi-automated fashion to generate more counts for each event. Hyphens were removed, plurals were converted to singular forms, finite verbs to infinitival forms, and gerundive nominals to verbs. Derivational ending on nominals were stripped and the corresponding infinitival verb form generated. These normalizations are rather aggressive and can lead to loss of important distinctions. For example, sets of events (e.g., storms or bombings) as a whole can have much longer durations compared to individual events. In addition, no word-sense disambiguation was carried out, so different senses of a given verb or event nominal may be confounded together.

5 Results

Number of durations	Number of Events	Normalized Form of Event
26	1	*lose*
16	1	*earn*
10	1	*fall*
9	1	*rise*
8	1	*drop*
7	2	*decline, increase*
6	4	*end, grow, say, sell*
5	2	*income, stop*
4	9	...
3	17	...
2	40	...
1	176	...

Table 1. Frequencies of event durations

The resulting dataset had 255 distinct events with the number of durations for the events as shown in the frequency distribution in Table 1. The granularities found in news corpora such as OTC and mixed corpora such as BNC are dominated by quarterly reports, which reflect the influence of specific information pinpointing the durations of financial events. This explains the fact that 12 of the top 13 events in Table 1 are financial ones, with the reporting verb *say* being the only non-financial event in the top 13.

The durations for the most frequent event, represented by the verb *to lose,* is shown in Table 2. Most losses are during a quarter, or a year, because financial news tends to quantize losses for those periods.

Duration	Frequency
1 day (P1D)	1
2 months (P2M)	1
unspecified weeks (PXW)	1
unspecified months (PXM)	1
3 months (P3M)	9
9 months (P9M)	3
1 year (P1Y)	6
5 years (P5Y)	1
1 decade (P1Y)	1
TOTAL	26

Table 2. Distribution of durations for event *to lose*

Ideally, we would be able to generalize over the duration values, grouping them into classes. Table 3 shows some hand-aggregated duration classes for the data. These classes are ranges of durations. It can be seen that the temporal span of events across the data is dominated by granularities of weeks and months, extending into small numbers of years.

Duration Class	Count
<1 min	1
5-15 min	12
1-<24 hr	20
1 day	14
2-14 days	49
1-3 months	120
7-9 months	48
1-6 years	97
1 decade - < 1 century	30
1-2 centuries	2
vague (unspecified mins/days/months, continuous present, indefinite future, etc.)	69

Table 3. Distribution of aggregated durations

Interestingly, 67 events in the data correspond to 'achievement' verbs, whose main characteristic is that they can have a near-instantaneous duration (though of course they can be iterated or extended to have other durations). We obtained a list of achievement verbs from the LCS lexicon of (Dorr and Olsen 1997)[3]. Achievements can be marked as having durations of PTXS, i.e., an unspecified number of seconds. Such values don't reinforce any of the observed values, instead extending the set of durations to include much smaller durations. As a result, these hidden values are not shown in our data

6 Estimating Duration Probabilities

Given a distribution of durations for events observed in corpora, one of the challenges is to arrive at an appropriate value for a given event (or class of events). Based on data such as Table 2, we could estimate the probability P(*lose*, P3M) ≅ 0.346, while P(*lose*, P1D) ≅ 0.038, which is nearly ten times less likely. Table 2 reveals peaking at 3 months, 6 months, and 9 months, with uniform probabilities for all others. Further, we can estimate the probability that losses will be during periods of 2 months, 3 months, or 9 months as ≅ 0.46. Of course, we would prefer a much large sample to get more reliable estimates.

One could also infer a max-min time range, but the maximum or minimum may not always be likely, as in the case of *lose*, which has relatively low probability of extending for "P1D" or "P1E". Turning to earnings, we find that P(*earn*, P9M) ≅ 4/16 = 0.25, P(*earn*, P1Y) ≅ 0.31, but P(*earn*, P3M) ≅ 0.43, since most earnings are reported for a quarter.

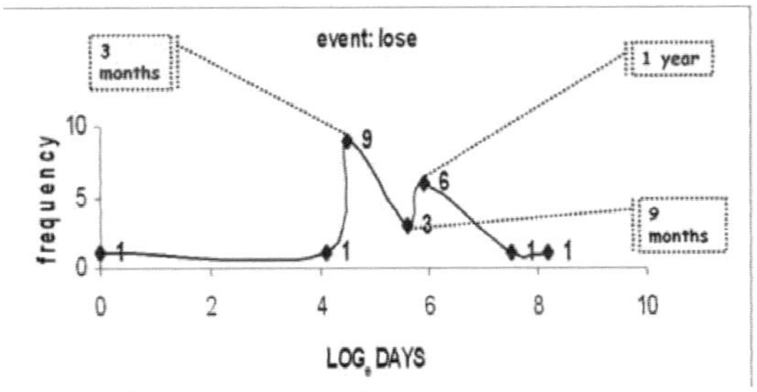

Figure 2. Distribution of durations of event *to lose*

So far, we have considered durations to be discrete, falling into a fixed number of categories. These categories could be atomic TimeML DU-

[3]See www.umiacs.umd.edu/ ~bonnie/ LCS_ Database_Documentation.html.

RATION values, as in the examples of durations in Table 2, or they could be aggregated in some fashion, as in Table 3. In the discrete view, unless we have a category of 4 months, the probability of a loss extending over 4 months is undefined. Viewed this way, the problem is one of classification, namely providing the probability that an event has a particular duration category.

The second view takes duration to be continuous, so the duration of an event can have any subinterval as a value. The problem here is one of regression. We can re-plot the data in Table 2 as Figure 2, where we have plotted durations in days on the x-axis in a natural log scale, and frequency on the y-axis. Since we have plotted the durations as a curve, we can interpolate and extrapolate durations, so that we can obtain the probability of a loss for 4 months. Of course, we would like to fit the best curve possible, and, as always, the more data points we have, the better.

7 Possible Enhancements

One of the basic problems with this approach is data sparseness, with few examples for each event. This makes it difficult to generalize about durations. In this section, we discuss enhancements that can address this problem.

7.1 Converting points to durations

More durations can be inferred from the OTC by coercing TIMEX3 DATE and TIME expressions to DURATIONS; for example, if someone announced something in 1997, the maximum duration would be one year. Whether this leads to reliable heuristics or not remains to be seen.

7.2 Event class aggregation

A more useful approach might be to aggregate events into classes, as we have done implicitly with financial events. Reporting verbs are already identified as a TimeML subclass, as are aspectual verbs such as *begin, continue* and *finish*. Arriving at an appropriate set of classes, based on distributional data or resource-derived classes (e.g., TimeML, VerbNet, WordNet, etc.) remains to be explored.

7.3 Expanding the corpus sample

Last but not least, we could expand substantially the search patterns and size of the corpus searched against. In particular, we could emulate the approach used in VerbOcean (Chklovski and Pantel 2004). This resource consists of lexical relations mined from Google searches. The mining uses a set of lexical and syntactic patterns to test for pairs of verbs strongly associated on the Web in a particular semantic relation. For example, the system discovers that *marriage* happens-before *divorce*, and that *tie* happens-before *untie*. Such results are based on estimating the probability of the joint occurrence of the two verbs and the pattern. One can imagine a similar approach being used for durations. Bootstrapping of patterns may also be possible.

8 Conclusion

This paper describes the first steps in acquiring metric temporal constraints for events. The work is carried out in the context of the TimeML framework for marking up events and their temporal relations. We have identified a method for enhancing TimeML annotations with metric constraints. Although the temporal reasoning required to carry that out has been described in the prior literature, e.g., (Kautz and Ladkin 1991), this is a first attempt at lexical acquisition of metrical constraints. As a pilot study, it does suggest the feasibility of acquisition of metric temporal constraints from corpora. In follow-on research, we will explore the enhancements described in Section 7.

However, this work is limited by the lack of evaluation, in terms of assessing how valid the durations inferred by our method are compared with human annotations. In ongoing work, Jerry Hobbs and his colleagues (Pan et al. 2006) have developed an annotation scheme for humans to mark up event durations in documents. Once such enhancements are carried out, it will certainly be fruitful to compare the duration probabilities obtained with the ranges of durations provided in that corpus.

In future, we will explore both regression and classification models for duration learning. In the latter case, we will investigate the use of constructive induction e.g., (Bloedorn and Michalski 1998). In particular, we will avail of operators to implement attribute abstraction that will cluster durations into coarse-grained classes, based on distributions of atomic durations observed in the data. We will also investigate the extent to which learned durations can be used to constrain TLINK ordering.

References

James Allen. 1984. Towards a General Theory of Action and Time. Artificial Intelligence, 23, 2, 123-154.

Eric Bloedorn and Ryszard S. Michalski. 1998. Data-Driven Constructive Induction. IEEE Intelligent Systems, 13, 2.

Branimir Boguraev and Rie Kubota Ando. 2005. TimeML-Compliant Text Analysis for Temporal Reasoning. Proceedings of IJCAI-05, 997-1003.

Timothy Chklovski and Patrick Pantel. 2004.VerbOcean: Mining the Web for Fine-Grained Semantic Verb Relations. Proceedings of EMNLP-04. http://semantics.isi.edu/ocean

B. Dorr and M. B. Olsen. Deriving Verbal and Compositional Lexical Aspect for NLP Applications. ACL'1997, 151-158.

Janet Hitzeman, Marc Moens and Clare Grover. 1995. Algorithms for Analyzing the Temporal Structure of Discourse. Proceedings of EACL'95, Dublin, Ireland, 253-260.

Feng Pan, Rutu Mulkar, and Jerry Hobbs. Learning Event Durations from Event Descriptions. Proceedings of Workshop on Annotation and Reasoning about Time and Events (ARTE'2006), ACL'2006.

C.H. Hwang and L. K. Schubert. 1992. Tense Trees as the fine structure of discourse. Proceedings of ACL'1992, 232-240.

Hans Kamp and Uwe Ryle. 1993. From Discourse to Logic (Part 2). Dordrecht: Kluwer.

Andrew Kehler. 2000. Resolving Temporal Relations using Tense Meaning and Discourse Interpretation, in M. Faller, S. Kaufmann, and M. Pauly, (eds.), Formalizing the Dynamics of Information, CSLI Publications, Stanford.

Henry A. Kautz and Peter B. Ladkin. 1991. Integrating Metric and Qualitative Temporal Reasoning. AAAI'91.

Mirella Lapata and Alex Lascarides. 2004. Inferring Sentence-internal Temporal Relations. In Proceedings of the North American Chapter of the Assocation of Computational Linguistics, 153-160.

Alex Lascarides and Nicholas Asher. 1993. Temporal Relations, Discourse Structure, and Commonsense Entailment. Linguistics and Philosophy 16, 437-494.

Wenjie Li, Kam-Fai Wong, Guihong Cao and Chunfa Yuan. 2004. Applying Machine Learning to Chinese Temporal Relation Resolution. Proceedings of ACL'2004, 582-588.

Inderjeet Mani and George Wilson. 2000. Robust Temporal Processing of News. Proceedings of ACL'2000.

Inderjeet Mani, Barry Schiffman, and Jianping Zhang. 2003. Inferring Temporal Ordering of Events in News. Short Paper. Proceedings of HLT-NAACL'03, 55-57.

Inderjeet Mani, Marc Verhagen, Ben Wellner, Chong Min Lee, and James Pustejovsky. 2006. Machine Learning of Temporal Relations. Proceedings of ACL'2006.

Rebecca J. Passonneau. A Computational Model of the Semantics of Tense and Aspect. Computational Linguistics, 14, 2, 1988, 44-60.

James Pustejovsky, Patrick Hanks, Roser Sauri, Andrew See, David Day, Lisa Ferro, Robert Gaizauskas, Marcia Lazo, Andrea Setzer, and Beth Sundheim. 2003. The TimeBank Corpus. Corpus Linguistics, 647-656.

James Pustejovsky, Bob Ingria, Roser Sauri, Jose Castano, Jessica Littman, Rob Gaizauskas, Andrea Setzer, G. Katz, and I. Mani. 2005. The Specification Language TimeML. In I. Mani, J. Pustejovsky, and R. Gaizauskas, (eds.), The Language of Time: A Reader. Oxford University Press.

Roser Saurí, Robert Knippen, Marc Verhagen and James Pustejovsky. 2005. Evita: A Robust Event Recognizer for QA Systems. Short Paper. Proceedings of HLT/EMNLP 2005: 700-707.

Frank Schilder and Christof Habel. 2005. From temporal expressions to temporal information: semantic tagging of news messages. In I. Mani, J. Pustejovsky, and R. Gaizauskas, (eds.), The Language of Time: A Reader. Oxford University Press.

Andrea Setzer and Robert Gaizauskas. 2000. Annotating Events and Temporal Information in Newswire Texts. Proceedings of LREC-2000, 1287-1294.

Marc Verhagen. 2004. Times Between The Lines. Ph.D. Dissertation, Department of Computer Science, Brandeis University.

Marc Verhagen, Inderjeet Mani, Roser Saurí, Robert Knippen, Jess Littman and James Pustejovsky. 2005. Automating Temporal Annotation with TARSQI. Demo Session, ACL 2005.

Marc Vilain, Henry Kautz, and Peter Van Beek. 1989. Constraint propagation algorithms for temporal reasoning: A revised report. In D. S. Weld and J. de Kleer (eds.), Readings in Qualitative Reasoning about Physical Systems, Morgan-Kaufman, 373-381.

Bonnie Webber. 1988. Tense as Discourse Anaphor. Computational Linguistics, 14, 2, 1988, 61-73.

Evaluating Knowledge-based Approaches to the Multilingual Extension of a Temporal Expression Normalizer

Matteo Negri
ITC-irst
Povo - Trento, Italy
negri@itc.it

Estela Saquete, Patricio Martínez-Barco, Rafael Muñoz
DLSI, University of Alicante
Alicante, Spain
{stela,patricio,rafael}@dlsi.ua.es

Abstract

The extension to new languages is a well known bottleneck for rule-based systems. Considerable human effort, which typically consists in re-writing from scratch huge amounts of rules, is in fact required to transfer the knowledge available to the system from one language to a new one. Provided sufficient annotated data, machine learning algorithms allow to minimize the costs of such knowledge transfer but, up to date, proved to be ineffective for some specific tasks. Among these, the recognition and normalization of temporal expressions still remains out of their reach. Focusing on this task, and still adhering to the rule-based framework, this paper presents a bunch of experiments on the automatic porting to Italian of a system originally developed for Spanish. Different automatic rule translation strategies are evaluated and discussed, providing a comprehensive overview of the challenge.

1 Introduction

In recent years, inspired by the success of MUC evaluations, a growing number of initiatives (*e.g.* TREC[1], CLEF[2], CoNLL[3], Senseval[4]) have been developed to boost research towards the automatic understanding of textual data. Since 1999, the Automatic Content Extraction (ACE) program[5] has been contributing to broaden the varied scenario of evaluation campaigns by proposing three main tasks, namely the recognition of *entities*, *relations*, and *events*. In 2004, the Timex2 Detection and Recognition task[6] (also known as TERN, for Time Expression Recognition and Normalization) has been added to the ACE program, making the whole evaluation exercise more complete. The main goal of the task was to foster research on systems capable of automatically detecting temporal expressions (TEs) present in an English text, and normalizing them with respect to a specifically defined annotation standard.

Within the above mentioned evaluation exercises, the research activity on monolingual tasks has gradually been complemented by a considerable interest towards multilingual and cross-language capabilities of NLP systems. This trend confirms how portability across languages has now become one of the key challenges for Natural Language Processing research, in the effort of breaking the language barrier hampering systems' application in many real use scenarios. In this direction, machine learning techniques have become the standard approach in many NLP areas. This is motivated by several reasons, including *i)* the fact that considerable amounts of annotated data, indispensable to train ML-based algorithms, are now available for many tasks, and *ii)* the difficulty, inherent to rule-based approaches, of porting language models from one language to new ones. In fact, while supervised ML algorithms can be easily extended to new languages given an annotated training corpus, rule-based approaches require to redefine the set of rules, adapting them to each new language. This is a time consuming and costly work, as it usually consists in manually rewriting from scratch huge amounts of rules.

[1] http://trec.nist.gov
[2] http://clef-campaign.org
[3] http://www.cnts.ua.ac.be/conll
[4] http://www.senseval.org
[5] http://www.nist.gov/speech/tests/ace
[6] http://timex2.mitre.org

Proceedings of the Workshop on Annotating and Reasoning about Time and Events, pages 30–37,
Sydney, July 2006.

In spite of their effectiveness for some tasks, ML techniques still fall short from providing effective solutions for others. This is confirmed by the outcomes of the TERN 2004 evaluation, which provide a clear picture of the situation. In spite of the good results obtained in the TE *recognition* task (Hacioglu et al., 2005), the *normalization* by means of ML techniques has not been tackled yet, and still remains an unresolved problem.

Considering the inadequacy of ML techniques to deal with the *normalization* problem, and focusing on portability across languages, this paper extends and completes the previous work presented in (Saquete et al., 2006b) and (Saquete et al., 2006a). More specifically, we address the following crucial issue: how to minimize the costs of building a rule-based TE recognition system for a new language, given an already existing system for another language. Our goal is to experiment with different automatic porting procedures to build temporal models for new languages, starting from previously defined ones. Still adhering to the rule-based paradigm, we analyse different porting methodologies that automatically learn the TE recognition model used by the system in one language, adjusting the set of normalization rules for the new target language.

In order to provide a clear and comprehensive overview of the challenge, an incremental approach is proposed. Starting from the architecture of an existing system developed for Spanish (Saquete et al., 2005), we present a bunch of experiments which take advantage of different knowledge sources to build an homologous system for Italian. Building on top of each other, such experiments aim at incrementally analyzing the contribution of additional information to attack the TE normalization task. More specifically, the following information will be considered:

- The output of online translators;
- The information mined from a manually annotated corpus;
- A combination of the two.

2 The task: TE recognition and normalization

The TERN task consists in automatically *detecting*, *bracketing*, and *normalizing* all the time expressions mentioned within an English text. The recognized TEs are then annotated according to the TIMEX2 annotation standard described in (Ferro et al., 2005). Markable TEs include both *absolute* (or *explicit*) expressions (*e.g.* "April 15, 2006"), and *relative* (or *anaphoric*) expressions (*e.g.* "three years ago"). Also markable are durations (*e.g.* "two weeks"), event-anchored expressions (*e.g.* "two days before departure"), and sets of times (*e.g.* "every week"). Detection and bracketing concern systems' capability to recognize TEs within an input text, and correctly determine their extension. Normalization concerns the ability of the system to correctly assign, for each detected TE, the correct values to the TIMEX2 normalization attributes. The meaning of these attributes can be summarized as follows:

- VAL: contains the normalized value of a TE (*e.g.* "2004-05-06" for "May 6th, 2004")
- ANCHOR_VAL: contains a normalized form of an anchoring date-time.
- ANCHOR_DIR: captures the relative direction-orientation between VAL and ANCHOR_VAL.
- MOD: captures temporal modifiers (possible values include: "approximately", "more_than", "less_than")
- SET: identifies expressions denoting sets of times (*e.g.* "every year").

2.1 The evaluation benchmark

Moving to a new language, an evaluation benchmark is necessary to test systems performances. For this purpose, the temporal annotations of the Italian Content Annotation Bank (I-CAB-temp[7]) have been selected.

I-CAB consists of 525 news documents taken from the Italian newspaper L'Adige (http://www.adige.it), and contains around 182,500 words. Its 3,830 temporal expressions (2,393 in the *training* part of the corpus, and 1,437 in the *test* part) have been manually annotated following the TIMEX2 standard with some adaptations to the specific morpho-syntactic features of Italian, which has a far richer morphology than English (see (Magnini et al., 2006) for further details).

[7] I-CAB is being developed as part of the three-year project ONTOTEXT funded by the Provincia Autonoma di Trento, Italy. See http://tcc.itc.it/projects/ontotext

3 The starting point: TERSEO

As a starting point for our experiments we used TERSEO, a system originally developed for the automatic annotation of TEs appearing in a Spanish written text in compliance with the TIMEX2 standard (see (Saquete, 2005) for a thorough description of TERSEO's main features and functionalities).

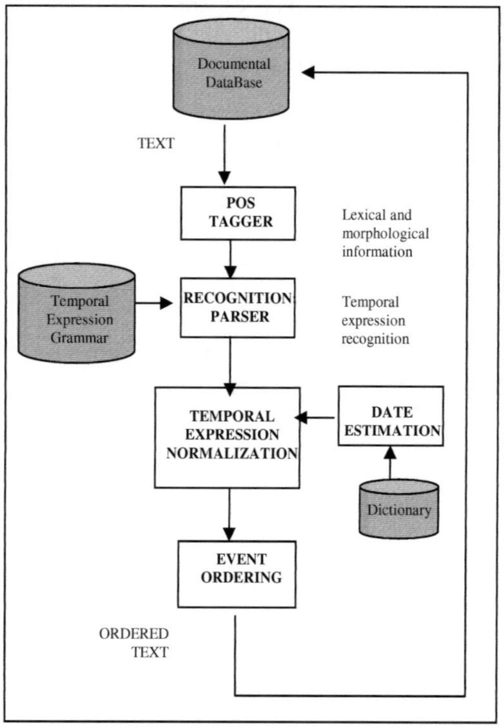

Figure 1: System's architecture.

Basically (see Figure 1), the TE recognition and normalization process is carried out in two phases. The first phase (recognition) includes a pre-processing of the input text, which is tagged with lexical and morphological information that will be used as input to a temporal parser. The temporal parser is implemented using an ascending technique (chart parser) and relies on a language-specific temporal grammar. As TEs can be divided into absolute and relative ones, such grammar is tuned for discriminating between the two groups. On the one hand, absolute TEs directly provide and fully describe a date. On the other hand, relative TEs require some degree of reasoning (as in the case of anaphora resolution).

In the second phase of the process, in order to translate these expressions into their normalized form, the lexical context in which they occur is considered. At this stage, a normalization unit is in charge of determining the appropriate reference date (anchor) associated to each *anaphoric* TE, calculating its value, and finally generating the corresponding TIMEX2 tag.

¿From a multilingual perspective, an important feature of TERSEO is the distinction between recognition rules, which are language-specific, and normalization rules, which are language-independent and potentially reusable for any other language. Taking the most from the modular architecture of the system, a first multilingual extension has been evaluated over the English TERN 2004 test set. In that extension, the English temporal model was automatically obtained from the Spanish one, through the automatic translation into English[8] of the Spanish TEs recognized by the system (Saquete et al., 2004). The resulting English TEs were then mapped onto the corresponding language-independent normalization rules, with good results (compared with other participants to the competition) both in terms of precision and recall. These results are shown in Table 1.

	Prec	Rec	F
timex2	0.673	0.728	0.699
anchor_dir	0.658	0.877	0.752
anchor_val	0.684	0.912	0.782
set	0.800	0.667	0.727
text	0.770	0.620	0.690
val	0.757	0.735	0.746

Table 1: Evaluation of *English*-TERSEO over the TERN 2004 test set

The positive results of this experience demonstrated the viability of the adopted solutions, and motivate our further investigation with Italian as a new target language.

4 Porting TERSEO to Italian

Due to the separation between language-specific recognition rules and language-independent normalization rules, the bulk of the porting process relies on the adaptation of the recognition rules to the new target language. Taking advantage of different knowledge sources (either alone or in combination), an incremental approach has been adopted, in order to determine the contribution of additional information on the performance of the resulting system for Italian.

[8] Altavista Babel Fish Translation has been used for this purpose (http://world.altavista.com).

4.1 Using online translators

As a first experiment, the same procedure adopted for the extension to English has been followed. This represents the simplest approach for porting TERSEO to other languages, and will be considered as a baseline for comparison with the results achieved in further experiments. The only minor difference with respect to the original procedure is that now, since two aligned sets of recognition rules (*i.e.* for Spanish and for English) are available, both models have been used. The reason for considering both models is the fact that they complement each other: on the one hand, the Spanish model was obtained manually and showed high precision values in detection (88%); on the other hand, although the English model showed lower precision results in detection (77%), the on-line translators from English to Italian perform better than translators from Spanish to Italian.

The process is carried out in the following four steps.

1. Eng-Ita translation. All the English TEs known by the system are translated into Italian[9]. Starting English, the probability of obtaining higher quality translations is maximized.

2. Spa-Ita translation. For each English TE without an Italian translation, the corresponding Spanish expression is translated into Italian. Also the Spanish TEs that do not have an English equivalent are translated from Spanish[10] into Italian. This way, the coverage of the resulting model is maximized, becoming comparable to the hand-crafted Spanish model.

3. TE Filtering. A filtering module is used to guarantee the correctness of the translations. For this purpose, the translated expressions are searched in the Web with Google. If an expression is not found by Google it is given up; otherwise it is considered as a valid Italian TE. The inconvenience of adopting this simple filtering strategy occurs in case of ambiguous expressions, *i.e.* when a correct expression is obtained through translation, and Google returns at least on document containing it, but the expression is not a temporal one. In these cases the system will erroneously store in its database non-temporal expressions. In this experiment the results returned by Google have not been analyzed (only the number of hits has been taken into account), nor the impact of these errors has been estimated. A more precise analysis of the output of the web search has been left as a future improvement direction.

4. Normalization rules assignment. Finally, the resulting Italian translations are mapped onto the language-independent normalization rules associated with the original English and Spanish TEs.

[9] Also for English to Italian translation, Altavista Babel Fish Translation has been used

[10] Using the Spanish-Italian translator available at http://www.tranexp.com:2000/Translate/result.shtml

The development of this first automatic porting procedure required one person/week for software implementation, and less than an hour to obtain the new model for Italian. The performance of the resulting system, evaluated over the test set of I-CAB, is shown in table 2.

	Prec	Rec	F
timex2	0.725	0.833	0.775
anchor_dir	0.211	0.593	0.311
anchor_val	0.203	0.571	0.300
set	0.152	1.000	0.263
text	0.217	0.249	0.232
val	0.364	0.351	0.357

Table 2: Porting to Italian based on translations

The results achieved by the translation-based approach are controversial. On the one hand, we observe a *detection* performance in line with the English version of the system. The **timex2** attribute, which indicates the proportion of detected TEs[11], has even higher scores, both in terms of precision (+5%) and recall (+11%), with respect to the English system. On the other hand, both *bracketing* (see the **text** attribute, which indicates the quality of extent recognition) and *normalization* (described by the other attributes) show a performance drop. Unfortunately, the reasons of this drop are still unclear. One possible explanation is that, due to the intrinsic difficulties presented by the Italian language, the translation-based approach falls short from providing an adequate coverage of the many possible TE variants. While

[11] At least one overlapping character in the extent of the reference and the system output is required for tag aligment.

the presence of *lexical triggers* denoting a TE appearing in a text (*e.g.* the Italian translations of "years", "Monday", "afternoon", "yesterday") can be easily captured by this approach, the complexity of many language-specific constructs is out of its reach.

4.2 Using an annotated corpus

In a second experiment, the annotations of the training portion of I-CAB have been used as a primary knowledge source. The main purpose of this approach is to maximize the coverage of the Italian TEs, starting from language-specific knowledge mined from the corpus. The basic hypothesis is that a *bottom-up* porting methodology, led by knowledge in the target language, is more effective than the *top-down* approach based on knowledge derived from models built for other languages. The former, in fact, is in principle more suitable to capture language-specific TE variations. In order to test the validity of ths hypothesis, the following two-step process has been set up:

1. TE Collection and translation. The Italian expressions are collected from the I-CAB training portion, and translated both into Spanish and English.

2. Normalization rules assignment. Italian TEs are assigned to the appropriate normalization rules. For each Italian TE mined from the corpus, the selection is done considering the normalization rules assigned to its translations. If both the Spanish and English expressions are found in their respective models, and are associated with the same normalization rule, then this rule is assigned also to the Italian expression. Also, when only one of the translated expressions is found in the existing models, the normalization rule is assigned. In case of discrepancies, *i.e.* if both expressions are found, but are not associated to the same normalization rule, then one of the languages must be prioritized. Since the manually obtained Spanish model has shown a higher precision, Spanish rules are preferred.

As the corpus-based approach is mostly built on the same software used for the translation-based porting procedure, it did not require additional time for implementation. Also in this case, the new model for Italian has been obtained in less than one hour. Performance results calculated over the I-CAB test set are reported in Table 3.

	Prec	**Rec**	**F**
timex2	0.730	0.839	0.781
anchor_dir	0.412	0.414	0.413
anchor_val	0.339	0.340	0.339
set	0.030	1.000	0.059
text	0.222	0.255	0.238
val	0.285	0.274	0.279

Table 3: Porting based on corpus annotations

These results partially confirm our working hypothesis, showing a performance increase in terms of the Italian TEs correctly recognized by the system. In fact, both the **timex2** attribute, which indicates the coverage of the system (detection), and the **text** attribute, which refers to the TEs extent determination (bracketing), are slightly increased. This may lead to the conclusion that automatic porting procedures can actually benefit from language-specific knowledge derived from a corpus.

However, looking at the other TIMEX2 attributes, the situation is not so clear due to the less coherent behaviour of the system on normalization. While for two attributes (**anchor_dir** and **anchor_val**) the system performs better, for the other two (**set** and **val**) a performance drop is observed. A possible reason for that could be related to the limited number of TE examples that can be extracted from the Italian corpus (whose dimensions are relatively small compared to the annotated corpora available for English). In fact, compared to the sum of English and Spanish examples used for the translation-based porting procedure, the Italian expressions present in the corpus are fewer and repetitive. For instance, with 131, 140, and 30 occurrences, the expressions "*oggi*" ("today"), "*ieri*" ("yesterday"), and "*domani*" ("tomorrow") represent around 12.5% of the 2,393 Italian TEs contained in the I-CAB training set.

4.3 Combining online translators and an annotated corpus

In light of the previous considerations, a third experiment has been conducted combining the *top-down* approach proposed in Section 4.1 and the *bottom-up* approach proposed in Section 4.2. The underlying hypothesis is that the induction of an effective temporal model for Italian can benefit from the combination of the large amount of examples coming from translations on the one side, and from the more precise language-specific knowledge derived from the corpus on the other.

To check the validity of this hypothesis, the process described in Section 4.2 has been modified adding an additional phase. In this phase, the set of TEs derived from I-CAB is augmented with the expressions already available in the Spanish and English TE sets. The new porting process is carried out in the following steps:

1. TE Collection and translation. The Italian expressions are collected from the I-CAB training portion, and translated both into Spanish and English.

2. Normalization rules assignment. With the same methodology described in Section 4.2 (step 2), the Italian TEs mined from the corpus are mapped onto the appropriate normalization rules assigned to their translations.

3. TE set augmentation. The set of Italian TEs is automatically augmented with new expressions derived from the Spanish and English TE sets. As described in Section 4.1, these expressions are first translated into Italian using on-line translators, then filtered through Web searches. The remaining TEs are included in the Italian model, and related to the same normalization rules assigned to the corresponding Spanish or English TEs.

Also this porting experiment was carried out with minimal modifications of the existing code. The automatic acquisition of the new model for Italian required around one hour. Evaluation results, calculated over the I-CAB test set are presented in Table 4.

	Prec	Rec	F
timex2	0.726	0.834	0.776
anchor_dir	0.578	0.475	0.521
anchor_val	0.516	0.424	0.465
set	0.182	1.000	0.308
text	0.258	0.296	0.276
val	0.564	0.545	0.555

Table 4: Porting based on corpus annotations and online translators

As can be seen from the table, the combination of the two approaches leads to an overall performance improvement with respect to the previous experiments. Apart from a slight decrease in terms of *detection* (**timex2** attribute), both bracketing and normalization performance benefit from such combination. The improvement on *bracketing* (**text** attribute) is around 4% with respect to both the previous experiments. On average, the improvement for the *normalization* attributes is around 15% with respect to the translation-based method (ranging from +4,5% for the **set** attribute, to +20% for the **val** attribute), and 20% with respect to the corpus-based method (ranging from +11% for the **anchor_dir** attribute, to +30% for the **set** attribute). These performance improvements are summarized in Table 5, which reports the F-Measure scores achieved by the three porting approaches.

	F-Tran.	F-Corpus	F-Comb.
timex2	0.775	**0.781**	0.776
anchor_dir	0.311	0.413	**0.521**
anchor_val	0.300	0.339	**0.465**
set	0.152	0.059	**0.308**
text	0.263	0.238	**0.276**
val	0.232	0.279	**0.555**

Table 5: F-Measure scores comparison

These results confirm the validity of our working hypothesis, showing that:

- taken in isolation, both the knowledge derived from models built for other languages, and the language-specific knowledge derived from an annotated corpus, have a limited impact on the system's performance;

- taken in combination, the *top-down* and the *bottom-up* approaches can complement each other, allowing to cope with the complexity of the porting task.

5 Comparing TERSEO with a language-specific system

For the sake of completeness, the results achieved by our combined porting procedure have been compared with those achieved, over the I-CAB test set, by a system specifically designed for Italian. The *ITA*-Chronos system (Negri and Marseglia, 2004), a multilingual system for the recognition and normalization of TEs in Italian and English, has been used for this purpose. Up to date, being among the two top performing systems at TERN 2004, Chronos represents the state-of-the-art with respect to the TERN task. In addition, to the best of our knowledge, this is the only system effectively dealing with the Italian language.

Like all the other state-of-the-art systems addressing the recognition/normalization task, *ITA*-Chronos is a rule-based system. From a design point of view, it shares with TERSEO a rather similar architecture which relies on different sets of rules. These are regular expressions that check for specific features of the input text, such as the presence of particular word senses, lemmas, parts of speech, symbols, or strings satisfying specific predicates[12]. Each set of rules is in charge of dealing with different aspects of the problem. In particular, a set of around 350 rules is designed for TE recognition and is capable of recognizing with high Precision/Recall rates a broad variety of TEs. Other sets of regular expressions, for a total of around 700 rules, are used in the normalization phase, and are in charge of handling each specific TIMEX2 normalization attribute. The results obtained by the Italian version of Chronos over the I-CAB test set are shown in Table 6.

	Prec	**Rec**	**F**	**F-Comb**
timex2	0.925	0.908	**0.917**	0.776 (-14%)
anchor_dir	0.733	0.636	**0.681**	0.521 (-16%)
anchor_val	0.495	0.462	**0.478**	0.465 (-1.3%)
set	0.616	0.500	**0.552**	0.308 (-24%)
text	0.859	0.843	**0.851**	0.276 (-57%)
val	0.636	0.673	**0.654**	0.555 (-10%)

Table 6: Evaluation of *ITA*-Chronos over the I-CAB test set

As expected, the distance between the results obtained by *ITA*-Chronos and the best Italian system automatically obtained from TERSEO (F-Comb) is considerable. On average, in terms of F-Measure, the scores obtained by *ITA*-TERSEO are 20% lower, ranging from -1.3% for the **anchor_val** attribute, to -57% for the **text** attribute. However, going beyond the raw numbers, a comprehensive evaluation must also take into account the great difference, in terms of the required time, effort, and resources deployed in the development of the two systems. While the implementation of the manual one took several months, the automatic porting procedure of TERSEO to Italian (in all the three modalities described in this paper) is a very fast process that can be accomplished in less than an hour. Considering the trade-off between performance and effort required for system's development, the proposed methodology represents a viable solution to attack the porting problem.

[12]For instance, the predicates "Weekday-p" and "Time_Unit-p" are respectively satisfied by strings such as "Monday", "Tuesday", ..., "Sunday", and "second", "minute", "hour", "day", ..., "century". Of course, this also holds for the Italian equivalents of these expressions

6 Conclusions

In this paper, the problem of automatically extending to new languages a rule-based system for TE recognition and normalization has been addressed. Adopting an incremental approach, different porting strategies, for the creation of an Italian system starting from an already available Spanish system, have been evaluated and discussed. Each experiment has been carried out considering the contribution of different knowledge sources for rules translation. Firstly, the contribution given by the output of online translators has been evaluated, showing detection performances in line with a previously developed English extension of the system, but a performance drop in terms of normalization performance. Then, the contribution of knowledge mined from an annotated corpus has been considered. Results show a performance increase in terms of detection and bracketing, but a less coherent behaviour in terms of normalization. Finally, a combined approach has been experimented, resulting in an overall performance increase. System's performance is still far from the results obtained by a state-of-the-art system for Italian but, considering the trade-off between performance and effort required for system's development, results are encouraging.

References

L. Ferro, L. Gerber, I. Mani, B. Sundheim, and G. Wilson. 2005. Tides.2005 standard for the annotation of temporal expressions. Technical report, MITRE.

K. Hacioglu, Y. Chen, and B. Douglas. 2005. Time Expression Labeling for English and Chinese Text. In *Proceedings of CICLing 2005*, pages 548–559.

B. Magnini, E. Pianta, C. Girardi, M. Negri, L. Romano, M. Speranza, and R. Sprugnoli. 2006. I-CAB: the Italian Content Annotation Bank. In *Proceedings of LREC 2006*. To appear.

M. Negri and L. Marseglia. 2004. Recognition and normalization of time expressions: Itc-irst at tern 2004. Technical report, ITC-irst, Trento.

E. Saquete, P. Martnez-Barco, and R. Muoz. 2004. Evaluation of the automatic multilinguality for time expression resolution. In *DEXA Workshops*, pages 25–30. IEEE Computer Society.

E. Saquete, R. Muoz, and P. Martnez-Barco. 2005. Event ordering using TERSEO system. *Data and*

Knowledge Engineering Journal, page (To be published).

E. Saquete, P. Martinez-Barco, R. Munoz R., M. Negri, M. Speranza, and R. Sprugnoli R. 2006a. Automatic resolution rule assignment to multilingual temporal expressions using annotated corpora. In *Proceedings of the TIME 2006 International Symposium on Temporal Representation and Reasoning*. To Appear.

E. Saquete, P. Martinez-Barco, R. Munoz R., M. Negri, M. Speranza, and R. Sprugnoli R. 2006b. Multilingual Extension of a Temporal Expression Normalizer using Annotated Corpora. In *Proceedings of the EACL Workshop on Cross-Language Knowledge Induction*.

E. Saquete. 2005. *Temporal information Resolution and its application to Temporal Question Answering*. Phd, Departamento de Lenguages y Sistemas Informáticos. Universidad de Alicante, June.

Extending TimeML with Typical Durations of Events

Feng Pan, Rutu Mulkar, and Jerry R. Hobbs
Information Sciences Institute (ISI), University of Southern California
4676 Admiralty Way, Marina del Rey, CA 90292, USA
{pan, rutu, hobbs}@isi.edu

Abstract

In this paper, we demonstrate how to extend TimeML, a rich specification language for event and temporal expressions in text, with the implicit typical durations of events, temporal information in text that has hitherto been largely unexploited. Event duration information can be very important in applications in which the time course of events is to be extracted from text. For example, whether two events overlap or are in sequence often depends very much on their durations.

1 Introduction

Temporal information processing has become more and more important in many natural language processing (NLP) applications, such as question answering (Harabagiu and Bejan, 2005; Moldovan et. al., 2005; Saurí et. al., 2005), summarization (Mani and Schiffman, 2005), and information extraction (Surdeanu et. al., 2003).

Temporal anchoring and event ordering are among the most important kinds of temporal information needed for NLP applications. Although there has been much work on extracting and inferring such information from texts (Hitzeman et al., 1995; Mani and Wilson, 2000; Filatova and Hovy, 2001; Boguraev and Ando, 2005), none of this work has exploited the implicit event duration information from the text.

Consider the sentence from a news article:

George W. Bush <u>*met*</u> *with Vladimir Putin in Moscow.*

How long was the meeting? Our first reaction to this question might be that we have no idea. But in fact we do have an idea. We know the meeting was longer than 10 seconds and less than a year. How much tighter can we get the bounds to be? Most people would say the meeting lasted between an hour and three days.

There is much temporal information in text that has hitherto been largely unexploited, encoded in the descriptions of events and relying on our knowledge of the range of usual durations of types of events, which can be very important in applications in which the time course of events is to be extracted from news. For example, whether two events overlap or are in sequence often depends very much on their durations. If a war started yesterday, we can be pretty sure it is still going on today. If a hurricane started last year, we can be sure it is over by now.

To extract such implicit event duration information from texts automatically, we developed a corpus annotated with typical durations of events (Pan et al., 2006a) which currently contains all the 48 non-Wall-Street-Journal (non-WSJ) news articles (a total of 2132 event instances), as well as 10 WSJ articles (156 event instances), from the TimeBank corpus annotated in TimeML (Pustejovky et al., 2003).

Because the annotated corpus is still fairly small, we cannot hope to learn to make *fine-grained* judgments of event durations that are currently annotated in the corpus, but as we show in greater detail in (Pan et al., 2006b), it is possible to learn useful *coarse-grained* judgments that considerably outperform a baseline and approach human performance.

This paper describes our work on extending TimeML with annotations of typical durations of events, which can enrich the expressiveness of TimeML, and provides NLP applications that exploit TimeML with this additional implicit event duration information for their temporal information processing tasks.

In Section 2 we first describe the corpus of typical durations of events, including the annotation guidelines, the representative event classes with examples, the inter-annotator agreement

Proceedings of the Workshop on Annotating and Reasoning about Time and Events, pages 38–45,
Sydney, July 2006.

study, and the machine learning results. TimeML and its event classes will be described in Section 3, and we will discuss how to integrate event duration annotations into TimeML in Section 4.

2 Annotating and Learning Typical Duration of Events

In the corpus of typical durations of events, every event to be annotated was already identified in the TimeBank corpus. Annotators are asked to provide lower and upper bounds on the duration of the event, and a judgment of level of confidence in those estimates on a scale from one to ten. An interface was built to facilitate the annotation. Graphical output is displayed to enable us to visualize quickly the level of agreement among different annotators for each event. For example, here is the output of the annotations (3 annotators) for the "finished" event (in bold) in the sentence

After the victim, Linda Sanders, 35, had ***finished*** *her cleaning and was waiting for her clothes to dry,...*

```
Event "finished":

s          mi         hr
|---------|---------|-------
          ====      1: [1 mi, 5 mi]
======              2: [1 s, 10 s]
    ============    3: [5 s, 10 mi]
```

This graph shows that the first annotator believes that the event lasts for minutes whereas the second annotator believes it could only last for several seconds. The third annotates the event to range from a few seconds to a few minutes. A logarithmic scale is used for the output.

2.1 Annotation Instructions

Annotators are asked to identify upper and lower bounds that would include 80% of the possible cases, excluding anomalous cases.

The judgments are to be made in context. First of all, information in the syntactic environment needs to be considered before annotating, and the events need to be annotated in light of the information provided by the entire article. Annotation is made easier and more consistent if coreferential and near-coreferential descriptions of events are identified initially.

When the articles were completely annotated by the three annotators, the results were analyzed and the differences were reconciled. Differences in annotation could be due to the differences in interpretations of the event; however, we found that the vast majority of radically different judgments can be categorized into a relatively small number of classes. Some of these correspond to aspectual features of events, which have been intensively investigated (e.g., Vendler, 1967; Dowty, 1979; Moens and Steedman, 1988; Passonneau, 1988). We then developed guidelines to cover those cases (see the next section).

2.2 Event Classes

Action vs. State: Actions involve change, such as those described by words like "speaking", "gave", and "skyrocketed". States involve things staying the same, such as being dead, being dry, and being at peace. When we have an event in the passive tense, sometimes there is an ambiguity about whether the event is a state or an action. For example,

Three people were ***injured*** *in the attack.*

Is the "injured" event an action or a state? This matters because they will have different durations. The state begins with the action and lasts until the victim is healed. Besides the general diagnostic tests to distinguish them (Vendler, 1967; Dowty, 1979), another test can be applied to this specific case: Imagine someone says the sentence after the action had ended but the state was still persisting. Would they use the past or present tense? In the "injured" example, it is clear we would say "Three people *were* injured in the attack", whereas we would say "Three people *are* injured from the attack." Our annotation interface handles events of this type by allowing the annotator to specify which interpretation he is giving. If the annotator feels it's too ambiguous to distinguish, annotations can be given for both interpretations.

Aspectual Events: Some events are aspects of larger events, such as their start or finish. Although they may seem instantaneous, we believe they should be considered to happen across some interval, i.e., the first or last *sub-event* of the larger event. For example,

After the victim, Linda Sanders, 35, had ***finished*** *her cleaning and was waiting for her clothes to dry,...*

The "finished" event should be considered as the last sub-event of the larger event (the "cleaning" event), since it actually involves opening the door of the washer, taking out the clothes, closing the door, and so on. All this takes time. This interpretation will also give us more information on typical durations than simply assuming such events are instantaneous.

Reporting Events: These are everywhere in the news. They can be direct quotes, taking exactly as long as the sentence takes to read, or they can be summarizations of long press conferences. We need to distinguish different cases:

Quoted Report: This is when the reported content is quoted. The duration of the event should be the actual duration of the utterance of the quoted content. The time duration can be easily verified by saying the sentence out loud and timing it. For example,

"It looks as though they panicked," a detective ***said*** *of the robbers.*

This probably took between 1 and 3 seconds; it's very unlikely it took more than 10 seconds.

Unquoted Report: This is when the reporting description occurs without quotes that could be as short as just the duration of the actual utterance of the reported content (lower bound), and as long as the duration of a briefing or press conference (upper bound).

If the sentence is very short, then it's likely that it is one complete sentence from the speaker's remarks, and a short duration should be given; if it is a long, complex sentence, then it's more likely to be a summary of a long discussion or press conference, and a longer duration should be given. For example,

The police ***said*** *it did not appear that anyone else was injured.*

A Brooklyn woman who was watching her clothes dry in a laundromat was killed Thursday evening when two would-be robbers emptied their pistols into the store, the police ***said.***

If the first sentence were quoted text, it would be very much the same. Hence the duration of the "said" event should be short. In the second sentence everything that the spokesperson (here the police) has said is compiled into a single sentence by the reporter, and it is unlikely that the spokesperson said only a single sentence with all this information. Thus, it is reasonable to give longer duration to this "said" event.

Multiple Events: Many occurrences of verbs and other event descriptors refer to multiple events, especially, but not exclusively, if the subject or object of the verb is plural. For example,

Iraq has ***destroyed*** *its long-range missiles.*

Both single (i.e., destroyed one missile) and aggregate (i.e., destroyed all missiles) events happened. This was a significant source in disagreements in our first round of annotation. Since both judgments provide useful information, our current annotation interface allows the annotator to specify the event as multiple, and give durations for both the single and aggregate events.

Events Involving Negation: Negated events didn't happen, so it may seem strange to specify their duration. But whenever negation is used, there is a certain class of events whose occurrence is being denied. Annotators should consider this class, and make a judgment about the likely duration of the events in it. In addition, there is the interval during which the nonoccurrence of the events holds. For example,

He was willing to withdraw troops in exchange for guarantees that Israel would not be ***attacked.***

There is the typical amount of time of "being attacked", i.e., the duration of a single attack, and a longer period of time of "*not* being attacked". Similarly to multiple events, annotators are asked to give durations for both the event negated and the negation of that event.

Positive Infinite Durations: These are states which continue essentially forever once they begin. For example,

He is ***dead.***

Here the time continues for an infinite amount of time, and we allow this as an annotation.

2.3 Inter-Annotator Agreement

Although the graphical output of the annotations enables us to visualize quickly the level of agreement among different annotators for each event, a quantitative measurement of the agreement is needed. The kappa statistic (Krippendorff, 1980; Carletta, 1996) has become the de facto standard to assess inter-annotator agreement. It is computed as:

$$\kappa = \frac{P(A) - P(E)}{1 - P(E)}$$

$P(A)$ is the observed agreement among the annotators, and $P(E)$ is the expected agreement,

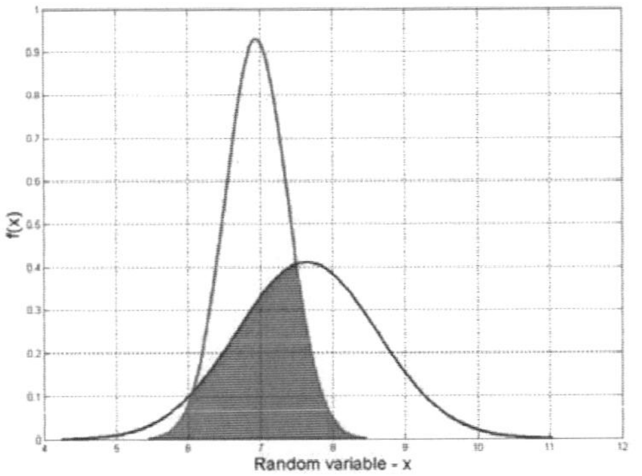

Figure 1: Overlap of Judgments of [10 minutes, 30 minutes] and [10 minutes, 2 hours].

which is the probability that the annotators agree by chance.

2.3.1 What Should Count as Agreement?

Determining what should count as agreement is not only important for assessing inter-annotator agreement, but is also crucial for later evaluation of machine learning experiments.

We first need to decide what scale is most appropriate. One possibility is just to convert all the temporal units to seconds. However, this would not correctly capture our intuitions about the relative relations between duration ranges. For example, the difference between 1 second and 20 seconds is significant; while the difference between 1 year 1 second and 1 year 20 seconds is negligible. In order to handle this problem, we use a logarithmic scale for our data. After first converting from temporal units to seconds, we then take the natural logarithms of these values. This logarithmic scale also conforms to the half orders of magnitude (HOM) (Hobbs and Kreinovich, 2001) which was shown to have utility in several very different linguistic contexts.

In the literature on the kappa statistic, most authors address only category data; some can handle more general data, such as data in interval scales or ratio scales (Krippendorff, 1980; Carletta, 1996). However, none of the techniques directly apply to our data, which are ranges of durations from a lower bound to an upper bound.

In fact, what coders were instructed to annotate for a given event is not just a range, but a *duration distribution* for the event, where the area between the lower bound and the upper bound covers about 80% of the entire distribution area. Since it's natural to assume the most likely duration for such distribution is its mean (average) duration, and the distribution flattens out toward the upper and lower bounds, we use the

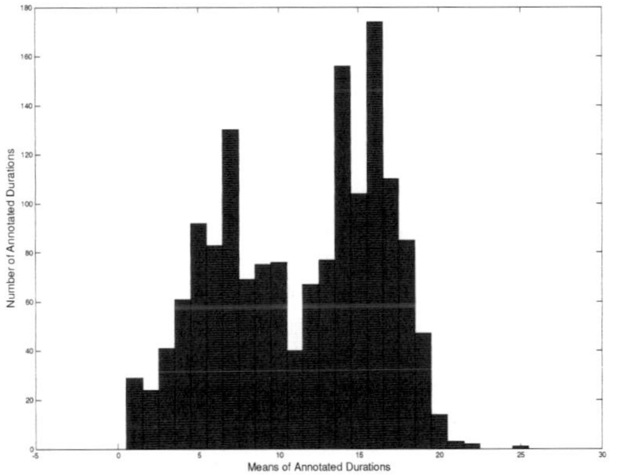

Figure 2: Distribution of Means of Annotated Durations.

normal or Gaussian distribution to model our duration distributions.

In order to determine a normal distribution, we need to know two parameters: the mean and the standard deviation. For our duration distributions with given lower and upper bounds, the mean is the average of the bounds. Under the assumption that the area between lower and upper bounds covers 80% of the entire distribution area, the lower and upper bounds are each 1.28 standard deviations from the mean.

With this data model, the agreement between two annotations can be defined as the overlapping area between two normal distributions. The agreement among many annotations is the average overlap of all the pairwise overlapping areas. For example, the overlap of judgments of [10 minutes, 30 minutes] and [10 minutes, 2 hours] are as in Figure 1. The overlap or agreement is 0.508706.

2.3.2 Expected Agreement

As in (Krippendorff, 1980), we assume there exists one global distribution for our task (i.e., the duration ranges for all the events), and "chance" annotations would be consistent with this distribution. Thus, the baseline will be an annotator who knows the global distribution and annotates in accordance with it, but does not read the specific article being annotated. Therefore, we must compute the global distribution of the durations, in particular, of their means and their widths. This will be of interest not only in determining expected agreement, but also in terms of what it says about the genre of news articles and about fuzzy judgments in general.

We first compute the distribution of the means of all the annotated durations. Its histogram is shown in Figure 2, where the horizontal axis

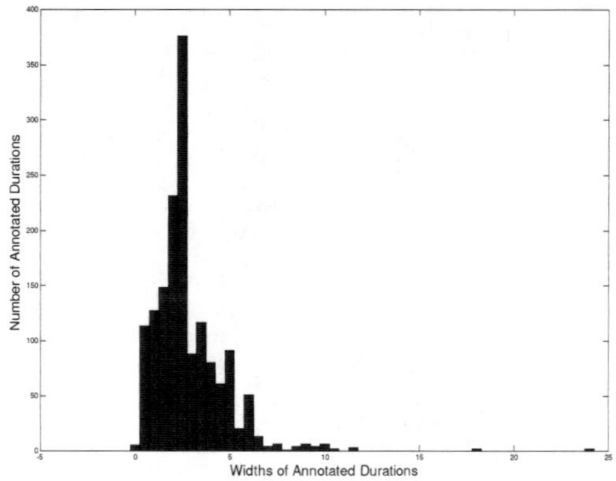

Figure 3: Distribution of Widths of Annotated Durations.

represents the mean values in the natural logarithmic scale and the vertical axis represents the number of annotated durations with that mean.

We also compute the distribution of the widths (i.e., upper bound – lower bound) of all the annotated durations, and its histogram is shown in Figure 3, where the horizontal axis represents the width in the natural logarithmic scale and the vertical axis represents the number of annotated durations with that width.

Two different methods were used to compute the expected agreement (baseline), both yielding nearly equal results. These are described in detail in (Pan et al., 2006a). For both, P(E) is about 0.15.

Experimental results show that the use of the annotation guidelines resulted in about 10% improvement in inter-annotator agreement, measured as described in this section, see (Pan et al., 2006a) for details.

2.4 Machine Learning Experiments

2.4.1 Features

Local Context. For a given event, the local context features include a window of *n* tokens to its left and *n* tokens to its right, as well as the event itself. The best *n* was determined via cross validation. A token can be a word or a punctuation mark. For each token in the local context, including the event itself, three features are included: the original form of the token, its lemma (or root form), and its part-of-speech (POS) tag.

Syntactic Relations. The information in the event's syntactic environment is very important in deciding the durations of events. For a given event, both the head of its subject and the head of its object are extracted from the parse trees generated by the CONTEX parser (Hermjakob and Mooney, 1997). Similarly to the local context features, for both the subject head and the object head, their original form, lemma, and POS tags are extracted as features.

WordNet Hypernyms. Events with the same hypernyms may have similar durations. But closely related events don't always have the same direct hypernyms. We extract the hypernyms not only for the event itself, but also for the subject and object of the event, since events related to a group of people or an organization usually last longer than those involving individuals, and the hypernyms can help distinguish such concepts. For our learning experiments, we extract the first 3 levels of hypernyms from WordNet (Miller, 1990).

2.4.2 Learning Coarse-grained Binary Event Durations

The distribution of the means of the annotated durations in Figure 2 is bimodal, dividing the events into those that take less than a day and those that take more than a day. Thus, in our first machine learning experiment, we have tried to learn this *coarse-grained* event duration information as a binary classification task.

Data. The original annotated data can be straightforwardly transformed for this binary classification task. For each event annotation, the most likely (mean) duration is calculated first by averaging (the logs of) its lower and upper bound durations. If its most likely (mean) duration is less than a day (about 11.4 in the natural logarithmic scale), it is assigned to the "short" event class, otherwise it is assigned to the "long" event class. (Note that these labels are strictly a convenience and not an analysis of the meanings of "short" and "long".)

We divide the total annotated non-WSJ data (2132 event instances) into two data sets: a training data set with 1705 event instances (about 80% of the total non-WSJ data) and a held-out test data set with 427 event instances (about 20% of the total non-WSJ data). The WSJ data (156 event instances) is kept for further test purposes.

Results. The learning results in Figure 4 show that among all three learning algorithms explored (Naïve Bayes (NB), Decision Trees C4.5, and Support Vector Machines (SVM)), SVM with linear kernel achieves the best overall precision (76.6%). Compared with the baseline (59.0%) and human agreement (87.7%), this level of performance is very encouraging, especially as the learning is from such limited training data.

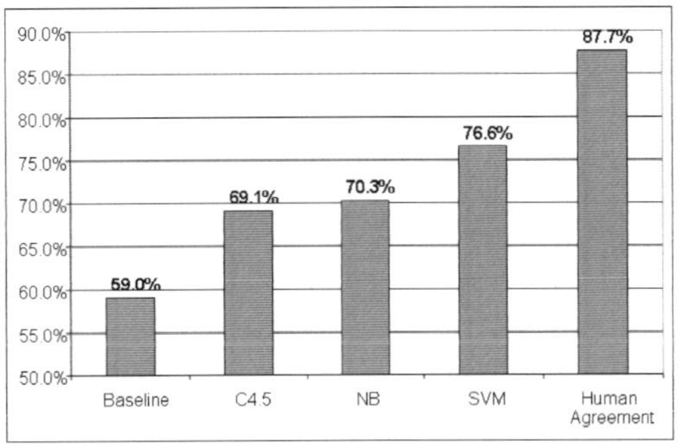

Figure 4: Overall Test Precision on non-WSJ Data.

Feature evaluation in (Pan et al., 2006b) shows that most of the performance comes from event word or phrase itself. A significant improvement above that is due to the addition of information about the subject and object. Local context does not help and in fact may hurt, and hypernym information also does not seem to help. It is gratifying to see that the most important information is that from the predicate and arguments describing the event, as our linguistic intuitions would lead us to expect.

In order to evaluate whether the learned model can perform well on data from different news genres, we tested it on the unseen WSJ data (156 event instances). A precision of 75.0%, which is very close to the test performance on the non-WSJ data, proves the great generalization capacity of the learned model.

Some preliminary experimental results of learning the more fine-grained event duration information, i.e., the most likely temporal unit (cf. (Rieger 1974)'s ORDERHOURS, ORDERDAYS), are shown in (Pan et al., 2006b). SVM again achieves the best performance with 67.9% test precision (baseline 51.5% and human agreement 79.8%) in "approximate agreement" where temporal units are considered to match if they are the same temporal unit or an adjacent one.

3 TimeML and Its Event Classes

TimeML (Pustejovsky et al., 2003) is a rich specification language for event and temporal expressions in natural language text. Unlike most previous attempts at event and temporal specification, TimeML separates the representation of event and temporal expressions from the anchoring or ordering dependencies that may exist in a given text.

TimeML includes four major data structures: EVENT, TIMEX3, SIGNAL, AND LINK. EVENT is a cover term for situations that happen or occur, and also those predicates describing states or circumstances in which something obtains or holds true. TIMEX3, which extends TIMEX2 (Ferro, 2001), is used to mark up explicit temporal expressions, such as time, dates, and durations. SIGNAL is used to annotate sections of text, typically function words that indicate how temporal objects are related to each other (e.g., "when", "during", "before"). The set of LINK tags encode various relations that exist between the temporal elements of a document, including three subtypes: TLINK (temporal links), SLINK (subordination links), and ALINK (aspectual links).

Our event duration annotations can be integrated into the EVENT tag. In TimeML each event belongs to one of the seven event classes, i.e., reporting, perception, aspectual, I-action, I-state, state, occurrence. TimeML annotation guidelines[1] give detailed description for each of the classes:

Reporting. This class describes the action of a person or an organization declaring something, narrating an event, informing about an event, etc (e.g., say, report, tell, explain, state).

Perception. This class includes events involving the physical perception of another event (e.g., see, watch, view, hear).

Aspectual. In languages such as English and French, there is a grammatical device of aspectual predication, which focuses on different facets of event history, i.e., initiation, reinitiation, termination, culmination, continuation (e.g., begin, stop, finish, continue).

I-Action. An I-Action is an Intensional Action. It introduces an event argument (which must be in the text explicitly) describing an action or situation from which we can infer something given its relation with the I-Action (e.g., attempt, try, promise).

I-State. This class of events are similar to the previous class. This class includes states that refer to alternative or possible worlds (e.g., believe, intend, want).

State. This class describes circumstances in which something obtains or holds true (e.g., on board, kidnapped, peace).

Occurrence. This class includes all the many other kinds of events describing something that happens or occurs in the world (e.g., die, crash, build, sell).

[1]http://www.cs.brandeis.edu/~jamesp/arda/time/timeMLdocs/annguide12wp.pdf

4 Integrating Event Duration Annotations into TimeML

Our event duration annotations can be integrated into TimeML by adding two more attributes to the EVENT tag for the lower bound and upper bound duration annotations (e.g., "lowerBoundDuration" and "upperBoundDuration" attributes).

To minimize changes of the existing TimeML specifications caused by the integration, we can try to share as much as possible our event classes as described in Section 2.2 with the existing ones in TimeML as described in Section 3.

We can see that four event classes are shared with very similar definitions, i.e., reporting, aspectual, state, and action/occurrence. For the other three event classes that only belong to TimeML (i.e., perception, I-action, I-state), the I-action and perception classes can be treated as special subclasses of the action/occurrence class, and the I-state class as a special subclass of the state class.

However, there are still three classes that only belong to the event duration annotations (i.e., multiple, negation, and positive infinite). The positive infinite class can be treated as a special subclass of the state class with a special duration annotation for positive infinity.

Each multiple event has two annotations. For example, for

Iraq has ***destroyed*** *its long-range missiles.*

there is the time it takes to destroy one missile and the duration of the interval in which all the individual events are situated – the time it takes to destroy all its missiles.

Since the single event is usually more likely to be encountered in multiple documents, and thus the duration of the single event is usually more likely to be shared and re-used, to simplify the specification, we can take only the duration annotation of the single events for the multiple event class, and the single event can be assigned with one of the seven TimeML event classes. For example, the "destroyed" event in the above example is assigned with the occurrence class in TimeBank.

The events involving negation can be simplified similarly. Since the event negated is usually more likely to be encountered in multiple documents, we can take only the duration annotation of the negated event for this class. For example, in

He was willing to withdraw troops in exchange for guarantees that Israel would not be ***attacked****.*

the event negated is the "being attacked" event and it is assigned with the occurrence class in TimeBank. Alternatively, TimeML could be extended to treat negations of events as states.

The format used for annotated durations is consistent with that for the value of the DURATION type in TimeML. For example, the sentence

The official ***said*** *these sites could only be* ***visited*** *by a special team of U.N. monitors and diplomats.*

can be marked up in TimeML as:

```
The official <EVENT eid="e63"
class="REPORTING"> said </EVENT>
these sites <SIGNAL sid="s65"
>could</SIGNAL> only be <EVENT
eid="e64" class="OCCURRENCE">
visited </EVENT> by a special team
of <ENAMEX TYPE="ORGANIZATION"> U.N.
</ENAMEX> monitors and diplomats.
```

If we annotate the "said" event with the duration annotation of [5 seconds, 5 minutes], and the "visited" event with [10 minutes, 1 day], the extended mark-up becomes:

```
The official <EVENT eid="e63"
class="REPORTING" lowerBoundDura-
tion="PT5S" upperBoundDura-
tion="PT5M"> said </EVENT> these
sites <SIGNAL sid="s65"
>could</SIGNAL> only be <EVENT
eid="e64" class="OCCURRENCE" lower-
BoundDuration="PT10M" upperBoundDu-
ration="P1D"> visited </EVENT> by a
special team of <ENAMEX
TYPE="ORGANIZATION"> U.N. </ENAMEX>
monitors and diplomats.
```

5 Conclusion

In this paper we have demonstrated how to extend TimeML with typical durations of events. We can see that the extension is very straightforward. Other interesting temporal information can be extracted or learned. For example, for each event class, we can generate its own mean and widths graphs, and learn their durations separately from other classes, which may capture different duration characteristics associated with each event class.

Acknowledgments

This work was supported by the Advanced Research and Development Activity (ARDA), now the Disruptive Technology Office (DTO), under DOD/DOI/ARDA Contract No. NBCHC040027. The authors have profited from discussions with Hoa Trang Dang, Donghui Feng, Kevin Knight, Daniel Marcu, James Pustejovsky, Deepak Ravichandran, and Nathan Sobo.

References

B. Boguraev and R. K. Ando. 2005. TimeML-Compliant Text Analysis for Temporal Reasoning. In *Proceedings of the International Joint Conferenceon Artificial Intelligence (IJCAI)*.

J. Carletta. 1996. Assessing agreement on classification tasks: the kappa statistic. *Computational Lingustics*, 22(2):249–254.

D. R. Dowty. 1979. *Word Meaning and Montague Grammar*, Dordrecht, Reidel.

L. Ferro. 2001. Instruction Manual for the Annotation of Temporal Expressions. Mitre Technical Report MTR 01W0000046, *the MITRE Corporation*, McLean, Virginia.

E. Filatova and E. Hovy. 2001. Assigning Time-Stamps to Event-Clauses. *Proceedings of ACL Workshop on Temporal and Spatial Reasoning*.

S. Harabagiu and C. Bejan. 2005. Question Answering Based on Temporal Inference. In *Proceedings of the AAAI-2005 Workshop on Inference for Textual Question Answering*, Pittsburgh, PA.

U. Hermjakob and R. J. Mooney. 1997. Learning Parse and Translation Decisions from Examples with Rich Context. In *Proceedings of the 35th Annual Meeting of the Association for Computational Linguistics (ACL)*.

J. Hitzeman, M. Moens, and C. Grover. 1995. Algorithms for Analyzing the Temporal Structure of Discourse. In *Proceedings of EACL*. Dublin, Ireland.

J. R. Hobbs and V. Kreinovich. 2001. Optimal Choice of Granularity in Commonsense Estimation: Why Half Orders of Magnitude, In *Proceedings of Joint 9th IFSA World Congress and 20th NAFIPS International Conference*, Vacouver, British Columbia.

K. Krippendorf. 1980. *Content Analysis: An introduction to its methodology*. Sage Publications.

I. Mani and G. Wilson. 2000. Robust Temporal Processing of News. In *Proceedings of Annual Conference of the Association for Computational Linguistics (ACL)*.

I. Mani and B. Schiffman. 2005. Temporally Anchoring and Ordering Events in News. In J. Pustejovsky and R. Gaizauskas ed. *Time and Event Recognition in Natural Language*. John Benjamins.

G. A. Miller. 1990. WordNet: an On-line Lexical Database. *International Journal of Lexicography* 3(4).

M. Moens and M. Steedman. 1988. Temporal Ontology and Temporal Reference. *Computational Linguistics* 14(2): 15-28.

D. Moldovan, C. Clark, and S. Harabagiu. 2005. Temporal Context Representation and Reasoning. In *Proceedings of the International Joint Conferenceon Artificial Intelligence (IJCAI)*.

F. Pan, R. Mulkar, and J. R. Hobbs. 2006a. An Annotated Corpus of Typical Durations of Events. To appear in *Proceedings of the Fifth International Conference on Language Resources and Evaluation (LREC)*, Genoa, Italy.

F. Pan, R. Mulkar, and J. R. Hobbs. 2006b. Learning Event Durations from Event Descriptions. To appear in *Proceedings of the 44th Conference of the Association for Computational Linguistics (COLING-ACL)*, Sydney, Australia.

R. J. Passonneau. 1988. A Computational Model of the Semantics of Tense and Aspect. *Computational Linguistics* 14:2.44-60.

J. Pustejovsky, J. Castano, R. Ingria, R. Saurí, R. Gaizauskas, A. Setzer, and G. Katz. 2003. TimeML: Robust specification of event and temporal expressions in text. In *Proceedings of the AAAI Spring Symposium on New Directions in Question-Answering*.

C. J. Rieger. 1974. Conceptual memory: A theory and computer program for processing and meaning content of natural language utterances. *Stanford AIM-233*.

R. Saurí, R. Knippen, M. Verhagen and J. Pustejovsky. 2005. Evita: A Robust Event Recognizer for QA Systems. In *Proceedings of HLT/EMNLP*.

M. Surdeanu, S. Harabagiu, J. Williams, and P. Aarseth. 2003. Using predicate-argument structures for information extraction. In *Proceedings of the 41th Annual Conference of the Association for Computational Linguistics (ACL-03)*, pages 8–15.

Z. Vendler. 1967. *Linguistics in Philosophy*, Ithaca, Cornell University Press.

Marking Time in Developmental Biology: Annotating Developmental Events and their Links with Molecular Events

Gail Sinclair
School of Informatics
University of Edinburgh
Edinburgh EH8 9LW
c.g.sinclair@ed.ac.uk

Bonnie Webber
School of Informatics
University of Edinburgh
Edinburgh EH8 9LW
bonnie@inf.ed.ac.uk

Duncan Davidson
MRC Human Genetics Unit
Western General Hospital
Edinburgh EH4 2XU
Duncan.Davidson@hgu.mrc.ac.uk

Abstract

Current research in developmental biology aims to link developmental genetic pathways with the processes going on at cellular and tissue level. Normal processes will only take place under specific sequential conditions at the level of the pathways. Disrupting or altering pathways may mean disrupted or altered development.

This paper is part of a larger work exploring methods of detecting and extracting information on developmental events from free text and on their relations in space and time.

1 Introduction

Most relation extraction work to date on biomedical articles has focused on genetic and protein interactions, e.g. the extraction of the fact that expression of Gene A has an effect on the expression of Gene B. However where genetic interactions are tissue- or stage-specific, the conditions that govern the types of interactions often depend on *where* in the body the interaction is happening (space) and *at what stage* of life/development (time).

For genetic pathways involved in development, it is critical to link what is happening at the molecular level to changes in the developing tissues, usually described in terms of processes such as *tubulogenesis* and *epithelialization* (both involved in the development of the kidney) and where they are happening.

The processes themselves are usually linked to *stages* rather than precise time points and spans like "6.15pm EST", "March 3", "last year". Within the developmental mouse community, there are at least two different ways of specifying the developmental stage of an embryo - Theiler stages (TS), and days post coitum/embryonic day (d.p.c./E). However, these cannot be simply mapped to one another as can days, weeks and years. Embryonic days are real time stages independent of the state of the embryo and dated from an assumption about when (approximately) the relevant coitus must have taken place, while Theiler stages are relative stages dependent on the processes an embryo is undergoing.

Developmental stages can be also be referred to implicitly, by the state of the embryo or the processes currently taking place within it. This is because during development, tissues form, change, merge or even disappear. So if the embryo is undergoing *tubulogenesis*, one can assume that its developmental stage is (loosely) somewhere between TS20 and birth. If the text refers to *induced mesenchyme* during a description of tubulogenesis, one can assume that this change in the mesenchyme is the (normal) consequence of the *Wolffian duct* invading the *metanephric mesenchyme*. The invasion is known to occur around 10.5 d.p.c so the *induced mesenchyme* must come into existence soon after this time.

Temporal links between developmental events may be indicated explicitly (e.g. *first, a tubule develops into a comma-shaped body, which then develops into an S-shaped body*), but they are more likely to be indicated implicitly by their ordering in the text and by associative (or "bridging") anaphora where the anaphor refers to the result of a previously mentioned process, e.g. the *induction of metanephric mesenchyme* as one event, and a subsequent mention of *induced mesenchyme* (an "associative" or "bridging" reference) within another event, suggesting the former event occurred before the latter.

Proceedings of the Workshop on Annotating and Reasoning about Time and Events, pages 46–53,
Sydney, July 2006.

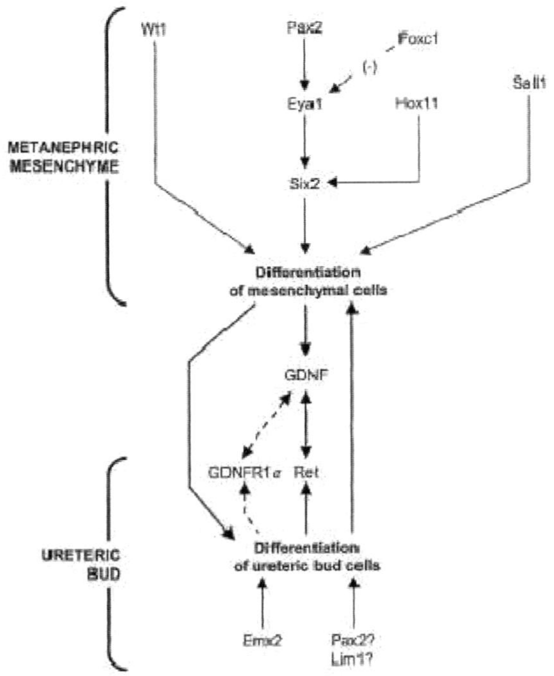

Figure 1: Partial genetic pathway for early kidney morphogenesis. The arrows show directed interactions between genes that are required for the specified processes. E.g Pax2 interacts with *(activates)* Six2 which, together with Sall1 and Wt1, is required for differentiation of the mesenchymal cells in the metanephric mesenchyme. Image taken from (Ribes et al., 2003).

This work on linking molecular and developmental events mentioned in text on development is also meant to deal with the problem that no one article ever fully describes a topic. The partial genetic interaction network in Figure 1 has been built from several different studies and not determined from just a single experiment. So not only does the information within one article need to be mined for useful information - the information across articles needs to be associated with each other with respect to temporal, spatial and experimental grounding. Eccles et al. (2002) states that Pax2 is required for differentiation of mesenchymal cells during kidney morphogenesis, while Sajithlal et al. (2005) states that Eya1 is required. However these two results by themselves do not help us determine whether these requirements are independent of one another or whether they are required at different stages or in different parts of metanephric mesenchyme or whether the two genes interact. The conditions involved in the experiments, most importantly the temporal conditions, can help to link the two events.

This work aims to develop methods for extracting information from text that will ground genetic pathways (molecular events) with regard to tissue location, developmental process and stage of embryonic development - that is, their **spatio-temporal context**. The task at hand is to recognise how biologists write about developmental events and then adapt existing or formulate new natural language processing techniques to extract these events and temporally relate them to each other. The resultant information can then be used both for database curation purposes and for visualisation, i.e. to enrich pathway diagrams such as Figure 1, with information such as when and where the interactions take place, what type of interactions are involved (physical, activation, inhibition), the origin of this information and other associated information.

2 Notions of Time

As previously mentioned, there are different ways of calibrating for developmental stages, and they cannot simply be mapped to one another. The two most common stage notations for mouse development are Theiler stages, TS, and Embryonic days, E (equivalent to days post coitum, d.p.c.). The latter are self explanatory in that they denote the 24 hour day and can be considered *real-time* staging.

The convention was originally that *E11* would represent the 24 hour period of the 11th day. It is, however, now common to find *E11.5* representing the same time period, but this is merely a change in convention due to standard practices of experimentation.

A Theiler stage on the other hand represents a non-fixed *relative* time period defined by the progress of development rather than directly in terms of the passage of time. Theiler Stages (Theiler, 1989) divide mouse development into 26 prenatal and 2 postnatal stages. In general, Theiler used external features that can be directly assessed by visual inspection of the live embryo as developmental landmarks to define stages. The Edinburgh Mouse Atlas Project (EMAP)[1] uses Theiler stages to organise anatomical terms in their Mouse Atlas Nomenclature (MAN). EMAP gives a brief description of each Theiler stage with TS25 as an example as follows:

> Skin wrinkled
> The skin has thickened and formed wrinkles and the subcutaneous veins are less visible. The fingers and toes have become parallel and the umbilical hernia has disappeared. The eyelids have fused. Whiskers are just visible.
> Absent: ear extending over auditory meatus, long whiskers.

An embryo is in TS25 at approximately 17 d.p.c. As can be seen in Figure 2, an embryo at E11 could be considered in Theiler stage 17, 18 or 19, i.e. Theiler stages can overlap one another with respect to Embryonic day. Indeed, here, TS17 can fully encompass TS18 in the dpc timeline.

The development of internal structures is approximately correlated with external developments, so except for fine temporal differences, the Theiler stages can be assumed to apply to the whole embryo. Theiler stages provide only gross temporal resolution of developmental events, and the development of internal structures often take place within the boundaries of one of these stages or overlapping stage boundaries. Thus, internal developmental processes can also have their own finer *relative* timeline or staging.

There is no ontology or reference book that comprehensively specifies this finer staging and the knowledge of the biologist as the reader of articles is relied upon. This work will contribute to making this deeper staging criteria explicit.

[1]Edinburgh Mouse Atlas Project - http://genex.hgu.mrc.ac.uk/

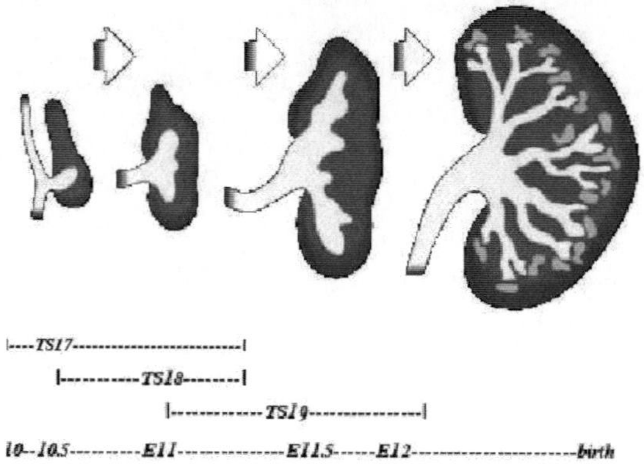

Figure 2: Graphic of kidney morphogenesis annotated with the two standard staging notations for mouse development. At E10.5 the Wolffian duct invades the metanephric mesenchyme forming the ureteric bud around E11. The bud then branches around E11.5 and continues to do so until birth, forming the ultimate functional units of the kidney - the nephrons. TS = Theiler Stage, E = Embryonic day/dpc. This image is adapted from http://www.sciencemuseum.org.uk/

3 Annotation

3.1 Event Classification

As a first step, a Gold Standard corpus of 988 sentences was developed with each sentence being classified as containing the description of a developmental and/or molecular event or not. 385 sentences were classified as positive, with 603 negative. Named entities within all these sentences were also annotated. Among these element types were *stage, process and tissue*. A Naive Bayes automatic classifier for sentence classification was developed using this Gold Standard resulting in a balanced F-score of 72.3% for event classification. (A manual rule-based approach resulted in an F-score of 86.6%, but this has yet to be fully investigated for automation. Guessing positive for all sentences would give a balanced F-score of 58.4%)

3.2 Event Specifications

Two event types are of interest in this work - *molecular* and *tissue* events. The former involve the action (and possible effect) of molecules during development and the latter involves the development of the tissues themselves. A description of an event can be expected to contain the following elements:

- *molecular* or *tissue* event type (e.g. *expression, inhibition*)
- stage or temporal expression (e.g. *after* X, *subsequent to* X, *E11*)
- at least one of
  - molecule name, anatomical term, biological process term

The informational elements included within an event description can then be used to relate events to each other. Specifically, processes involve known tissues and are known to happen during certain stages, just as the relative order of processes, tissue formations and stages are known.

While an initial specification of an event may be associated with a single sentence, clause or phrase, not all the elements of relevance to this work may be specified there. In particular, an informational element of the event may be explicitly and fully stated in this initial event specification, or it may be underspecified or it may be missing. For those that are underspecified or missing, background knowledge about other elements and events may need to be taken into consideration in order for them to be fully resolved (see Section 4.2).

The following is a straightforward example where the given sentence specifies all the main elements required for a molecular event.

1. *At E11, the integrin α8 subunit was expressed throughout the mesenchyme of the nephrogenic cord.*
   - Molecular Event : *expression*
   - molecule name: *integrin α8*
   - anatomical term: *mesenchyme of the nephrogenic cord*
   - stage: *E11*

Example 2 shows that a single sentence may specify more than one event.

2. *Prior to formation of the ureteric bud, no α8 expression was evident within the mesenchyme that separates the urogenital ridge from the metanephric mesenchyme and within the metanephric mesenchyme itself.*

- EVENT-0
  - Tissue Event : *formation of* anatomical term
  - anatomical term: *ureteric bud*
  - stage/temporal expression = missing
- EVENT-1
  - Molecular Event: absence of expression
  - molecule name: α*8*
  - anatomical term: *mesenchyme that separates the urogenital ridge from the metanephric mesenchyme*
  - temporal expression:*Prior to* EVENT-0
- EVENT-2
  - Molecular Event: absence of expression
  - molecule name: α*8*
  - anatomical term: *metanephric mesenchyme*
  - temporal expression: *Prior to* EVENT-0

EVENT-0 is not the focus of this sentence, but rather a *reference* event. Its attributes need to be recorded so that the stage of the other events can be determined.

TimeML (Pustejovsky et al., 2004) is a specification language designed for the annotation of temporal and event information. Although TimeML is not currently being used as a method of representation for this work, Example 1 above could be represented as follows:

<SIGNAL sid="s1" type="temporal">
At
</SIGNAL>
<TIMEX tid="t1" type="STAGE" value="E11">
E11
</TIMEX>
the integrin α8
<EVENT eid="e1" class="molecular">
was expressed
</EVENT>
throughout the mesenchyme of the
<SIGNAL sid="s2" type="tissue">
nephrogenic cord
</SIGNAL>
nephrogenic cord can be considered a signal of type "tissue" as it does not exist throughout the

whole of development and so can indicate or rule out time periods for this event description.

3.3 Event Time-Stamping

The relative timing of any biological processes mentioned in the event descriptions first needs to be determined before we can work out when the actual events described are taking place.

Schilder and Habel (2001) looked beyond the core temporal expressions and into prepositional phrases that contained temporal relations, i.e. *before, during*, etc and introduced the notion of noun phrases as event-denoting expressions. An event that is described as occurring "after the election" does not have an explicit time-stamp attached to it, but the knowledge about the timing of the election mentioned gives the reader a notion of when in absolute time the event occurred. This is similar to Example 2 above where Event-0 is the reference event, thus biological processes can be considered event-denoting expressions.

While Schilder and Habel rely on prepositional phrases to designate their event-denoting noun phrases, for this work propositional phrases are not necessarily required. The mention of a noun phrase by itelf may be enough. In developmental biology, tissues may only be extant for a limited period before they form into some other tissue and these can also be used as event-denoting expressions - for example, *comma-shaped bodies* are structures within the developing kidney that are only in existence for a relatively short time period - before the existence of the *S-shaped bodies* and after *epithelialization*. Therefore the mention of tissues as well as processes can help to pinpoint the timing of the event being described. While they may not ultimately bring us to the exact stage the event is occurring in, it can at least rule out some spans of time. We discuss this further in Section 4.2.

In order for events to be linked to one another, it is necessary to uniquely index each event and its elements. Mapping across indices will be utilised so that known relationships between elements can be represented. For example, E10 comes **before** E12, *tubulogenesis* occurs **during** *kidney morphogenesis*, and the *proximal tubule* is **part of** the *nephron*.

Of the elements types listed in Section 3.2, only the *molecule* element cannot be used to resolve developmental stage while *tissue, process, stage* and, of course, *temporal expression* can. Other elements are also of interest to the biologist and integral to development and molecular function, however they are not of use in the grounding of events in time.

4 Initial Investigations

This section demonstrates that one must look beyond the sentence in order to resolve the temporal aspects of events.

4.1 Evidence for Developmental Stage

Evidence sufficient to resolve developmental stage can come from many places. 314 positive sentences from the Gold Standard corpus and their context were examined, and the evidence required to resolve developmental stage for each of the events mentioned there was determined as shown in Table 1.

As can be seen from the table, only 48 out of the 314 event sentences (i.e. 15%) have the developmental stage in which the event is occurring *explicitly stated* in the given sentence, (e.g. Example 1 in Section 3). So other means need to be explored in order to ground events with respect to developmental stage. An event sentence may be a continuation of a topic, and so the specific developmental stage involved may well be stated in the immediately surrounding or related text.

Information in the immediately surrounding text (rows labelled *Following Sentence, Previous Sentence* and *Current Paragraph*) resolves the developmental stage of the event in 64 cases (i.e. 21%). This most commonly occurs by looking for the immediately previously mentioned stage, and in one case the next encountered stage.

Event sentences also often refer to figures, and so the stage being described in the caption (i.e. legend) of the referenced figure will often be the same as the one relevant to the sentence. (This was true of all sentences looked at that referenced a figure.) Figures, however, are generally only found in the *Results* sections and so this type of evidence is not often going to be of use for sentences found in other sections of an article.

Similarly, events can be described within the figure legends themselves. The concise and simple way in which legends are generally written mean that the explicit stage is commonly referred to, and so stage can be resolved using this referenced information(43 out of 47 cases, i.e. 91%).

Source of Evidence	Abstract	Introduction	Results	Discussion	Methods	Totals
Time Irrelevant	7	12	22	23	1	65
Prior Knowledge	17	33	31	45	0	126
Following Sentence	0	0	1	0	0	1
Previous Sentence	0	0	7	0	0	7
Current Paragraph	0	0	18	1	0	19
Reference to Figure	0	0	38	0	0	38
Within Fig Legend	0	0	43	0	0	43
(time not resolved)	0	3	1	0	0	4
Explicitly Stated	0	1	41	5	1	48
(not relevant)	0	0	1	0	0	1
Totals	24	49	165	74	2	314

Table 1: Location and type of evidence sufficient to resolve developmental stage in sentences. *Time Irrelevant* indicates that the event being described is not time critical, i.e. event is a constant over developmental timeline, or end result. *Prior knowledge* means temporal information other than that found in the current paragraph but associated with current event such as *tissue* and *process* is required for temporal resolution. This may be found in the current article or from previously curated information (assuming accurate terminology mapping.) Text from outside the current paragraph cannot be relied upon to be relevant to the current sentence without additional information. *time not resolved* means the stage could not be pinpointed using the figure legend. *not relevant* indicates that although an explicit stage was referred to within the sentence, this was not relevant to the event being described, e.g. event and stage in different clauses of the sentence.

Table 2 shows a similar table to Table 1, but deals only with those sentences found within figure legends. It shows where within the figure legend the required evidence for developmental stage can be found. As can be seen, in 80% of these cases the relevant developmental stage can be ascertained directly from the legend. It should be noted that figure legends in biological articles tend to be much lengthier than those from NLP articles.

In 21% of the event sentences, a specific developmental stage is not relevant to the fact being described (first row of Table 1), e.g. *the kidneys of the double mutants were located more caudal and medial than normal.* This sentence is describing an end result, i.e. an affected or normal kidney at birth (although this could, of course, be considered a developmental stage.) Alternatively, the time-irrelevant event being described could be a non-event, e.g. the fact that a gene is *never* expressed in a particular tissue. Similarly, this could be considered as the developmental stage range from conception to birth.

The significantly small proportion of event sentences located in Abstracts (24 of 314 total event sentences, less than 8%) demonstrates the need to use full text. Even where an event is described within an Abstract, it is rarely accompanied by associated processes or tissues specific enough to suggest the stage of development never mind an explicit timestamp, as it is, by necessity, only generally describing the whole article. The majority of BioNLP work is being done with the use of Abstracts only. This is because of their relative ease of access compared with full text, but methods developed using Abstracts only will not necessarily be as effective when applied to full text.

As can be seen, the majority of temporally-underspecified event sentences are situated in the *Results* section of the articles. Indeed, this is the section where most event sentences are to be found. This work is initially focussing on event descriptions found in Results sections of articles as these will focus on the work done by the authors and their findings and will not generally include modality in the event descriptions as Introduction and Discussion sections might. As shown above, the Methods section rarely contains event descriptions and when they do they are usually about what the experiment aims to show and so this should be repeated in the Results section.

4.2 Prior Knowledge

As mentioned earlier, if none of the above sources reveal the relevant stage of an event, then other elements within the sentence, such as *tissue* or *process*, need to be looked at so that prior knowledge

Source of Evidence	Figure Legends
Time Irrelevant	4
Prior Knowledge	4
Following Sentence	0
Previous Sentence	14
Current Paragraph	13
Explicitly Stated	11
Total	47

Table 2: Location and type of evidence sufficient to resolve developmental stage in sentences within figure legends. Rows as in Table 1, with *Current Paragraph* being equal to the whole of the legend.

about those elements can be exploited for developmental stage to be resolved. For example, given the sentence

> *Prior to formation of the ureteric bud, no α8 expression was evident within the mesenchyme that separates the urogenital ridge from the metanephric mesenchyme and within the metanephric mesenchyme itself.*

the developmental stage can be resolved if we know when the ureteric bud forms (TS17/E10.5). It could also be the case that the other tissues or processes mentioned have a specific lifetime within development and these could help to further pinpoint the timeline involved for the lack of *α8* expression. For example,

> *Pax2 was initiating in the metanephric mesenchyme undergoing induction.*

It is not so straightforward to assign a stage here, since the mesenchyme is constantly being induced from E11 (TS18) until birth (TS26), but we have at least discounted E1-E10 (TS1-TS17) as relevant stages.

Resources such as the Mouse Atlas Nomenclature (MAN) (Ringwald et al., 1994) will provide the initial prior knowledge in order to resolve developmental stage of events. This describes the different stages of development and the tissues in evidence at each stage, giving what is known as the *abstract mouse*. From this abstract mouse, we can ascertain the normal stage ranges where tissues exist and use this knowledge for temporal resolution, taking care not to assume that tissues do not necessarily exist within the same stage range in mutant mice than in wild-type. The prior knowledge databank can be recursively added to with facts from events already extracted from papers for use in further event extraction and their anchoring in time.

5 Future Work

5.1 Term Normalisation

There is no point extracting events descriptions if we cannot relate the events and their elements to each other. The event-denoting expressions identified need to be normalised so that it can be recognised when two terms are referring to the same element.

Inconsistent terminology in the biomedical field is a known problem (Sinclair et al., 2002). One gene can have several names (synonymy) just as the same name can be used for more than one gene (homonymy). Very often the synonyms bear no relation to one another since they were perhaps concurrently discovered in different laboratories and named. For example, the gene *insomnia* can also be known as *cheap date*, since experiments found that organisms without this gene have a tendency to fall asleep and are particularly susceptible to alcohol. The same anatomical part can also be referred to by different terms, e.g. the *Wolffian duct* is also known as the *nephric duct*, and the *metanephros* is another name for the *kidney*. There is also a lineage issue, where a tissue with one name (or perhaps more) develops into something with another name (e.g. the *intermediate mesoderm* gives rise to both the *Wolffian duct* and the *metanephric mesenchyme* which in turn both develop into the *metanephros*. The MAN includes this type of information.

Term normalisation is particularly important for the *process* and *tissue* elements. If these terms are not normalised, temporal knowledge about the terms may not be exploited and it may not be determined that events involving them are linked.

5.2 Event Elements

If the elements required to fully describe an event are explicitly stated within a simple sentence, then temporal grounding will be straightforward. However, this is unlikely to often be the case. More complex sentences will dictate the need for dependency relations to be determined so that each event's elements can be identified. Methods for dealing with missing or underspecified elements that are not resolved within the event description itself will be investigated.

A naive approach will first be investigated to fill these gaps: find the closest appropriate element in the previous context (varying the size of the window for how far back to look, such as current paragraph or last 3 sentences). An error analysis on this simple method will help to guide the amount of further work necessary to achieve equal success across all elements. For those elements that this method is ineffective, other methods will be developed incorporating features such as sensitivity to syntax, event type and location within article. Similarly, it will be established whether different techniques are required for missing information than for underspecified information. They will first be treated in the same manner with analysis determining whether they should be treated differently.

6 Conclusion

This ongoing work has shown the importance of relative time lines in order to link events to one another. The identification of event elements and their normalisation will then form a basis for reasoning over these elements with regards to first time-stamping of events and then temporally relating the events. The aim of many BioNLP studies is ultimately to reason over extracted events and, as such, the relative timing of these events is crucial. For example, if we know
1. tissue X is transformed into tissue Y at stage S and
2. molecule M is expressed in X at stage S-1,
then it can be reasoned that event 2 has an impact on event 1. This reasoning can be made more successful if we know as much about the events as possible, not just that tissue Y is formed and molecule M is expressed.

It has also been demonstrated that we not only need to look beyond the sentence level for temporal resolution but also beyond the article in order to replicate the reader's assumed level of background knowledge.

References

J. F. Allen, Towards a general theory of action and time, *Artificial Intelligence*, vol 23, pp 123-154, 1984.

M. R. Eccles, S. He, M. Legge, R. Kumar, J. Fox, C. Zhou, M. French and R. W. Tsai, .PAX genes in development and disease: the role of PAX2 in urogenital tract development. *Int J Dev Biol*, vol 46, no 4, pp 535-44, 2002.

J. Pustejovsky, I. Mani, L. Belanger, B. Bogurev, B. Knippen, J. Littman, A. Rumshisky, A. See, S. Symonen, J. Van Guilder, L. Van Guilder and M. Verhagen, The Specification Langeuage TimeML. in The Language of Time: A Reader, Oxford University Press, 2004.

D. Ribes, E. Fischer, A. Calmont and J. Rossert, Transcriptional Control of Epithelial Differentiation during Kidney Development. *J Am Soc Nephrol*, vol 14, pp S9-S15, 2003.

M. Ringwald, R. A. Baldock, J. Bard, M. H. Kaufman, J. T. Eppig, J. E. Richardson, J. H. Nadeau and D. Davidson, A database for mouse development. *Science*, vol 265, pp 2033-2034, 1994.

G. Sajithlal, D. Zou, D. Silvius and P. X. Xu, Eya 1 acts as a critical regulator for specifying the metanephric mesenchyme. *Dev Biol*, vol 284, no 2, pp 323-36, 2005.

F. Schilder and C. Habel, From Temporal Expressions to Temporal Information: Semantic Tagging of News Message., in *Proceedings of the ACL 2001 Workshop on Temporal and Spatial Information Processing, Toulouse, France*, pp 88-95.

G. Sinclair, B. Webber and D. Davidson, Enhanced Natural Language Access to Anatomically Indexed Data. in *Proceedings of the ACL 2002 Workshop on Natural Language Processing in the Biomedical Domain*, Philadelphia, pp 45-52.

K. Theiler, *The House Mouse. Atlas of Embryonic Development.* Springer Verlag New York, 1989.

Author Index

Association for Computational Linguistics
209 N. Eighth Street
Stroudsburg, Pennsylvania 18360

18th Conference on Computational Natural Language Learning

(CoNLL 2014)

Held in Conjunction with ACL 2014

Baltimore, Maryland, USA
26 – 27 June 2014

ISBN: 978-1-63439-230-3